Westward Expansion

THE MAKING OF AMERICA

Westward Expansion

Dale Anderson

JNF 978.02 ANDERSON

RAINTREE
STECK-VAUGHN
PUBLISHERS

A Harcourt Company

Austin • New York
www.steck-vaughn.com

Published by Raintree Steck-Vaughn Publishers, an imprint of Steck-Vaughn Company

Developed by Discovery Books
Editor: Sabrina Crewe
Designer: Sabine Beaupré
Maps: Stefan Chabluk

Raintree Steck-Vaughn Publishers Staff
Publishing Director: Walter Kossmann
Art Director: Max Brinkmann
Editor: Shirley Shalit

Consultant Andrew Frank, California State University, Los Angeles

Library of Congress Cataloging-in-Publication Data
Anderson, Dale, 1953-
    Westward expansion / Dale Anderson.
        p. cm. -- (The making of America)
    Includes bibliographical references (p.) and index.
    ISBN 0-8172-5705-5
        1. West (U.S.)--Discovery and exploration--Juvenile literature. 2. West
(U.S.)--History--Juvenile literature. 3. Frontier and pioneer life--West (U.S.)--Juvenile
literature. 4. United States--Territorial expansion--Juvenile literature. [1. West
(U.S.)--Discovery and exploration. 2. United States--Territorial expansion.] I. Title. II.
Making of America (Austin, Tex.)
F591.A49 2000
978'.02-dc21
                                                                00-035753

Printed and bound in the United States of America
1 2 3 4 5 6 7 8 9 0 IP 05 04 03 02 01 00

Acknowledgments
Cover The Granger Collection; pp. 6, 7, 9, 14, 16, 17 The Granger Collection; p. 20 North Wind Picture Archives; p. 22 © Harry Jackson, 1980; p. 24 North Wind Picture Archives; pp. 26, 27, 29 Corbis; pp. 33, 35 The Granger Collection; p. 40 Corbis; p. 42 The Granger Collection; p. 44 Corbis; p. 47 Seaver Center for Western History Research, Los Angeles County Museum of Natural History; p. 48 Corbis; p. 49 North Wind Picture Archives; p. 52 The Granger Collection; p. 53 Corbis; p. 54 The Granger Collection; pp. 56, 58 Corbis; pp. 59, 62 The Granger Collection; pp. 63, 65, 66, 67 Corbis; p. 68 The Granger Collection; p. 70 Corbis; pp. 71, 72 The Granger Collection; p. 73 Kansas State Historical Society; pp. 75, 76 The Granger Collection; p. 78 Buffalo Bill Historical Center, Cody, Wyoming; pp. 80, 81, 83 The Granger Collection; p. 84 Corbis; p. 86 Buffalo Bill Historical Center, Cody, Wyoming; p. 87 Autry Museum of Western Heritage, Los Angeles.

Cover illustration: This painting by William Henry Jackson shows a wagon train of the mid-1800s by the Sweetwater River at Devil's Gate, Wyoming, heading west on the Oregon Trail.

Contents

Introduction

"This is the country for a man to enjoy himself. . . . There is enough to spare of everything a person can desire."

Settler Samuel Crabtree, in a letter to his brother in England, 1818

To the white settlers who lived along the Atlantic coast in the 1700s, "the West" was just beyond the frontiers of their colonies. They did not know of the vast reaches of the Great Plains or the tall peaks of the Rocky Mountains. The West meant the area between the Appalachian Mountains and the Mississippi River. It stretched from the Great Lakes in the north to the Gulf of Mexico in the south.

The region had many resources. Wide rivers could be used for transportation. Plentiful deer and game birds provided meat. There was a lively trade in deerskins and beaver fur. Forests covered much of the land, but the soil was fertile.

In the British colonies along the coast, available land was becoming scarce. The abundant, fertile land in the West looked inviting to the white settlers. One observer in the 1700s, Nathaniel Ames, commented, "Now behold! The farmer may have . . . land enough for himself and all of his sons." However, the British colonists were not the only ones who wanted the West. Spanish and French settlers were already there. And thousands of Native Americans, gathered in many different tribes, lived in the area. There were years of conflict ahead.

In the 1700s, many Native American people of the West lived the way they had done for centuries. The land did not belong to them so much as they belonged to the land. As white people began moving into the region, this changed. The new settlers saw the land as something to be divided and owned.

6

The First Frontier

The region west of the Appalachians was home to many different peoples in the 1700s. French fur traders and settlers lived near the Great Lakes and along the Mississippi River. To the south were Spanish settlers. Of the Native Americans who lived there, some were newcomers to the area. They had been pushed over the mountains by the Europeans who had settled along the Atlantic coast. Other tribes had lived there for many generations.

Trade in the West

The different tribes had varied ways of life. Those in present-day Georgia, Alabama, and Mississippi—called by whites the "Five Civilized Tribes"—had a complex society based on growing corn and trading deerskins. Those in the Great Lakes region lived by hunting and fishing and growing corn or gathering wild rice. Many of these northern Indians formed a vital part of the profitable French fur trade. Indians caught beaver, trading the pelts to

A fur-trading post in about 1785. Fur traders stocked their posts with goods to trade with Indian fur trappers. In exchange for beaver fur, which was popular with white Americans and in Europe, the Indians received guns, cloth, and other items that had previously been unknown and unavailable to them.

the French for valuable goods such as guns and gunpowder, iron pots, wool and cotton cloth, and rum. French fur traders (who bought and sold the furs) and trappers (who caught animals for fur by setting traps) often married Native American women. This further united the two peoples. Trading posts—such as the one run by Jean Baptiste Pointe du Sable—became places of business and of peace.

Du Sable's trading post eventually grew to be the great city of Chicago. Another French trading post, strategically placed on the Mississippi River near where it is joined by the Missouri River, became the city of St. Louis.

Because of their flourishing trade, many Native American tribes saw the French as useful allies. The British were less appealing. They were more interested in taking the Indians'

Jean Baptiste Pointe du Sable (c.1745–1818)

Jean Baptiste Pointe du Sable was born in present-day Haiti, the son of a French ship owner and his African slave. When du Sable's mother died, his father sent him to Paris for schooling. He then worked on his father's ships, and came to North America either through Canada or Louisiana.

Du Sable became a fur trader in what is now Illinois. During the American Revolution, du Sable was arrested by the British for "treasonable intercourse with the enemy." Luckily, he was able to convince the British of his innocence. In fact, they hired him to manage their trading post.

Du Sable then met and married a woman of the Potawatomi tribe. In 1784, he and his wife settled on the banks of a river that fed Lake Michigan, where they established a trading post for fur trappers. The local Native Americans had named the river the "Checagou," after a chief of the Illinois Indians. From this site, modern Chicago grew. A plaque in Chicago's business district today marks the original location of du Sable's cabin.

Both Native Americans and whites were welcomed by du Sable, whose visitors included the Ottawa chief Pontiac and the pioneer Daniel Boone. Du Sable continued to build his holdings into a sizable settlement. He tried to win election as a chief of the local tribes, but lost. Du Sable ultimately sold his Chicago land and moved to Peoria, Illinois; and later to Missouri.

land than in trading with them. When the French and British fought a series of wars in the 1700s, Indians tended to side with the French. The last of those wars, the French and Indian War, ended in 1763 with British victory. France was forced, for the time being, to give up all its land in North America. Spain received the area around the southern part of the Mississippi River, including New Orleans, an important port. Britain took the rest of what was then the West, which meant it had control of the region from the Atlantic coast to the Mississippi River and up to the Great Lakes.

British Rule

Many Native Americans feared British rule would mean growing numbers of white settlers. Concern became anger, and soon much of the Great Lakes region was ablaze with war. Between May and June 1763, Indians attacked and destroyed several British forts. They wanted to force the British to recognize their right to the land. The strategy seemed to work. That fall, Britain passed a new law. The Proclamation of 1763 banned white people from settling west of the Appalachian Mountains. It even declared that any whites already living there had to move back east. To the British colonists along the Atlantic coast, the Proclamation was an outrage.

The region was too vast for the British to enforce the law, however. People continued to trickle over the mountains.

Daniel Boone led a group of settlers through the Cumberland Gap in 1769. They were on their way to the region the Indians called "ken-ta-ke," meaning "great meadow." Although the area, now the state of Kentucky, was then considered Indian land, white settlers kept coming along Boone's trail to claim the land for themselves.

9

Daniel Boone (1734–1820)

One of America's most famous pioneers, Daniel Boone was born to Quaker parents near Reading, Pennsylvania. Boone had little formal schooling, but he developed good frontier skills and became a hunter at the age of 12. Boone volunteered to fight with the British in the French and Indian War.

Boone's life was changed by hearing stories about Kentucky's wilderness. He made his first journey there in 1767–69, through the Cumberland Gap in the Allegheny Mountains. In 1775, Boone and a party of woodsmen cleared a path called the Wilderness Road, blazing a 250-mile (400-km) trail from North Carolina to Kentucky. Many settlers would use this road as their gateway to the West. During this trip, Boone also began the town of Boonesborough by building a fort. After a few more years in Kentucky, he journeyed to more remote territory, first in what is now West Virginia and then to present-day Missouri. Boone later became a symbol of the independent spirit of those who lived on the frontier.

They mostly settled in three areas: in present-day Kentucky; in what is now eastern Tennessee; and near what is now Pittsburgh, Pennsylvania. Wealthy Easterners tried to buy land, hoping to sell it at a profit. One landowner, Richard Henderson, hired a pioneer named Daniel Boone to lead a group to cut a trail from the colonies to Kentucky.

During the American Revolution, which began in 1775, the area west of the Appalachians became part of the battleground. Native Americans now sided with the British. They hoped to defeat the Americans and put an end to the spread of settlements. Fighting between the two sides was fierce and destructive. Harsh attacks by one side were avenged by the other, and the level of violence and bitterness grew.

While the battles raged, neither side gained a major advantage in this region. But after the war, the Americans won the prize they wanted. In the 1783 Treaty of Paris, the British recognized American independence. They also gave the new United States all the land between the Appalachian Mountains and the Mississippi River.

Organizing New Territories

The Continental Congress, which governed the United States, had to organize the land. It acted first in the area north of the Ohio River, the region known as the Northwest.

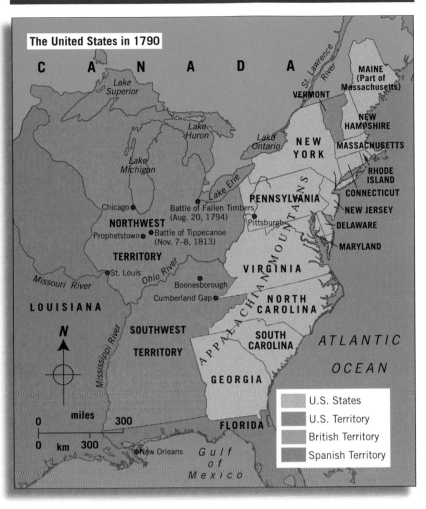

The United States in 1790

C A N A D A

Lake Superior

Lake Huron

Lake Michigan

Lake Ontario

Lake Erie

St. Lawrence River

MAINE (Part of Massachusetts)

VERMONT

NEW HAMPSHIRE

NEW YORK

MASSACHUSETTS

RHODE ISLAND

CONNECTICUT

NEW JERSEY

DELAWARE

MARYLAND

PENNSYLVANIA

Chicago

Battle of Fallen Timbers (Aug. 20, 1794)

Pittsburgh

NORTHWEST

Prophetstown ● Battle of Tippecanoe (Nov. 7–8, 1813)

TERRITORY

St. Louis

Ohio River

Missouri River

LOUISIANA

Boonesborough

Cumberland Gap

VIRGINIA

NORTH CAROLINA

APPALACHIAN MOUNTAINS

N

SOUTHWEST

TERRITORY

Mississippi River

SOUTH CAROLINA

GEORGIA

ATLANTIC OCEAN

miles

0   300

0   300
km

FLORIDA

New Orleans

Gulf of Mexico

U.S. States
U.S. Territory
British Territory
Spanish Territory

By 1790, the United States had claimed the areas known as the Northwest and the Southwest, which meant all the land between the original 13 states and the Mississippi River south of the Great Lakes. After the Land Ordinance of 1785 divided the Northwest into townships, white settlers arrived in ever-increasing numbers. Although many Native Americans tried to resist, they soon lost the battle against white expansion. The Indians signed over large areas of the West in treaties with the United States.

Congress passed two laws that set the rules for settling and governing these new territories.

The first of these, the Land Ordinance of 1785, ordered that the land be divided into townships, comprising 36 sections of 640 acres. The law said that the land would be sold at auction, a section at a time, for no less than one dollar an acre.

In 1787, the second law, the Northwest Ordinance, provided for the area to be divided into three to five territories. Those territories, after following a set procedure, could become states, equal in status to the original states. Within them, there would be freedom of worship, but slavery was prohibited.

> "The idea of being ultimately obliged to abandon their country rankles in [the Native Americans'] minds."
>
> *Arthur St. Clair, governor of the Northwest Territory*

11

The Contest for Control

The Northwest Ordinance pledged "the utmost good faith" toward the Native Americans in the region. It promised "their lands and property shall never be taken from them without their consent." But those promises would later be set aside.

The new laws did not lead to a flood of settlers. Buyers had to buy a whole section of 640 acres. That was more than a single family could farm, and $640 in cash was a huge sum in 1785. Those who bought land were wealthy people—some of them members of Congress—who usually tried to resell it.

Still, settlement did grow, and trouble arose again. When the British controlled the area, they had placed government agents with several tribes to keep good relations. According to the treaty that ended the American Revolution, the agents were supposed to be removed, but the British kept them at several sites. They encouraged the Indians to resist the American settlers.

Battles in the Northwest

In 1790, some American troops attacked native villages in Ohio. Native Americans under the Miami leader Little Turtle defeated those troops and a larger force commanded by Arthur St. Clair, governor of the Northwest Territory. In 1794, General Anthony Wayne fought with Native Americans at the Battle of Fallen Timbers in Ohio. Many Indians tried to find shelter in a nearby British fort. But the commander—unwilling to provoke another war between Britain and the United States—refused to let them in. The Native Americans were defeated.

After his victory, Wayne forced the Miami and other tribes to sign the Treaty of Greenville of 1814. In it, they handed over large amounts of land in Ohio. The United States government agreed to recognize the Indians' claim to the remaining land. Time would tell whether the government would honor its promise.

American Gains

While these events were taking place in the Northwest, Spain remained a power in what was then called the Southwest, along the lower Mississippi River valley. The Spanish, like the British, encouraged Native Americans to oppose American growth. By holding New Orleans, Spain controlled shipping on the Mississippi. This, in turn, gave them power over trade in the Northwest because the easiest way to ship goods from that region was down the Ohio and Mississippi Rivers. The Spanish taxed American goods heavily, and sometimes banned Americans from using the Mississippi altogether.

In 1795, the United States gained important ground. The British agreed by treaty to pull their agents out of the Northwest, and a treaty with Spain gave Americans the right to use the Mississippi River. Events in Europe had forced the British and Spanish to take these steps. Both nations were deeply involved in wars with France, and could not risk further tangles in North America.

Settling the Land

These changes had an effect on settlement also. After Fallen Timbers and the treaties with Britain and Spain, white settlers streamed into the Northwest. The entire population of the Cherokee—the largest tribe between the Appalachians and the Mississippi—was outnumbered by the settlers who came down the Ohio River in 1788 alone.

Another change also spurred people to move. With the Harrison Land Act of 1800, the rules for buying land shifted in favor of the small farmer. Lots of 320 acres could be bought, a better size for a family farm. And buyers only had to pay a quarter of the price in cash at the time of purchase. The rest could be paid over time.

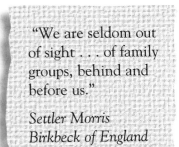

"We are seldom out of sight . . . of family groups, behind and before us."

Settler Morris Birkbeck of England

By 1800, the area that is now Ohio had more than 45,000 people. In just ten more years, the population jumped to more than 230,000, and in 1820 it was almost 600,000. The population of what is now Indiana grew as well, from about 24,500 in 1810 to almost 150,000 in 1820.

This picture shows the home of white settlers in Ohio in about 1831. Hundreds of thousands of settlers had come to the area since 1800, but it was still an isolated and difficult way of life. The settlers chopped their small farms out of the heavily forested land around them and built log homes from the trees they cleared.

Most settlers were families. Some traveled in wagons pulled by horses or oxen. Those less well off trudged along on foot. The journey complete, they had to create a farm. The first obstacle was the trees: "O the woods! the interminable woods!" wrote one person. They had to cut down trees, remove stumps, build homes, plant seeds, tend their fields, and harvest their crops. They also had to make many of the things they needed.

A different way of life arose in the Southwest. The invention of the cotton gin in 1793 speeded up cotton production. Southern cotton planters soon began moving from the coastal states to build huge plantations in what are now Alabama and Mississippi. They brought slavery with them. Others adopted cattle ranching from the Spanish and turned it into an important industry in the Southwest.

Cultural Changes

The growth of settlement created a blending of cultures. Whites adopted Native American foods such as corn and dried deer meat. They used the Indian technique of burning trees to fertilize the ground and made Indian medicines from local plants. They gave native names to many of their settlements and used many other Native American words.

Indians, in turn, adopted many aspects of European culture. Iron pots were efficient for cooking. Woven blankets kept people warm. Metal fish hooks lasted longer than those made of bone. Over time, Native Americans came to rely on white people's goods. And as white settlements spread, the Indians lost more of the land that provided the resources for their traditional ways of life.

Old Conflicts Renewed

In the midst of the white expansion westward, Native Americans tried to rally their forces. A Shawnee leader, Tecumseh, and his brother became the leaders of a new movement for Indian defense. Tecumseh's brother, known as "The Prophet," began to have mystical visions and teach a new religion. He took the name Tenskwatawa, which means "Open Door." Tenskwatawa had an appealing message: Follow his teachings, and the whites would disappear.

Tecumseh hoped to persuade all Native American tribes to stop giving up land. He wanted to avoid fighting, certainly until he had united all the Indian peoples. A few thousand followers gathered at Prophetstown, the brothers' camp on Tippecanoe Creek in what is now Indiana.

In November 1811, Tecumseh was away, trying to build support in the Southwest. William Henry Harrison, the governor of Indiana, led a force toward Prophetstown, and Tenskwatawa ordered his followers to attack. The soldiers easily defeated the Native Americans and destroyed the town.

During the War of 1812, Tecumseh joined forces with the British and fought in many battles. He was an able leader, but he died fighting in 1813 at the Battle of the Thames in Canada. Native American power in the Northwest was broken.

The War of 1812 touched the Native Americans of the Southwest as well. The Creek people had split into two

> "You alone shall inhabit the land."
>
> *Tenskwatawa to the Native American people*

The Battle of Tippecanoe in 1811 was the largest battle in the Northwest Territory for some years. Fearing Indian raids on white settlements in Indiana Territory, General Harrison had been preparing to attack Prophetstown. On November 7, Harrison's forces were surprised by an army of Shawnee Indians led by Tenskwatawa. But with their superior weapons, the Americans quickly overcame the Shawnee warriors.

groups, one hostile to whites and the other more friendly. Those who fiercely opposed white settlers called themselves the Red Sticks. They killed hundreds of the other group and white settlers in several clashes that became known as the Creek War. In March 1814, General Andrew Jackson led a force of soldiers and Cherokee allies against the Red Sticks in the Battle of Horseshoe Bend in what is now Alabama. Jackson's army killed hundreds of Red Sticks, shattering their strength and ending the Creek War.

The Indian Removal Act

Indian defeats in both northern and southern regions made the West even more appealing to white settlers. The pressure for land became intense, and those Native Americans who remained in the region became targets.

The "Five Civilized Tribes"—the Cherokee, Chickasaw, Choctaw, Creek, and Seminoles—held land in Florida, Georgia, Alabama, and Mississippi. These peoples adopted many features of white society. Sequoyah, born of a Cherokee mother and a white father, had created a written form of the Cherokee language by 1821. It was used to write a constitution for the Cherokee and to publish a newspaper. Cherokee men gave up hunting and took to farming, work traditionally done by women.

The governments of the southern states tried to pressure the Native Americans to leave. Congress passed the Indian Removal Act in 1830, which supplied money to buy the Indians' land. Many Native Americans did agree to sell their land and move west of the Mississippi. The Cherokee, however, tried to fight the move.

In the 1830s, the Cherokee took their case to the United States Supreme Court. In an important decision, the Court ruled that state laws had no effect on land held by the tribe. The Cherokee victory meant nothing, though. Andrew Jackson, now president of the United States, favored the removal of the Indians and defied the Supreme Court decision. His agents convinced a small group of Cherokee to sign away the tribe's land. Most Cherokee did not recognize the treaty, but Jackson sent the army to enforce it.

The Trail of Tears

From 1830 to 1838, almost all the members of the Five Civilized Tribes moved west. One group of Cherokee, however, remained in the Smoky Mountains of North

> "We . . . humbly petition our beloved children, the head men of warriors, to hold out to the last in support of our common rights. . . . We claim the right of the soil."
>
> *Petition of Cherokee women to male leaders, 1818*

In 1838, after being held for several months in removal camps, the Cherokee began their journey west, on the Trail of Tears. Food and medicine, promised by the government, were rarely supplied, and thousands died on the trail.

> "Even aged females, apparently nearly ready to drop in the grave, were traveling with heavy burdens attached to their backs, sometimes on frozen ground and sometimes on muddy streets, with no covering for their feet."
>
> *An observer of the Trail of Tears*

Carolina. The federal government gave them a reservation there, west of the city of Asheville, where their people still live today.

At first, the Seminoles of Florida also did not make the move. Osceola, a Seminole chief, led them in a long war against the United States. The American army finally abandoned the fight in 1842. By then, many Seminoles had moved west, although others remained in Florida.

Native Americans who did move were forced to accept land in the "Indian Territory," a large area of land west of the Mississippi. In 1838, many thousands of Cherokee people started on the long, harsh trail to the Indian Territory, most of them coming from Georgia. Perhaps a quarter of them never arrived, having died along the way from starvation, disease, or exposure to extreme weather. This terrible journey became known as "The Trail of Tears."

Varied Lives, Common Ideas

Before white settlers came to North America, traditional ways of life differed widely. The Cherokee of the Southwest and the Pueblo tribes of the Spanish Southwest were farming peoples who lived in settled communities. The peoples of the Pacific Northwest lived by catching sea mammals and fishing for salmon. The Plains peoples farmed and hunted the large, roaming herds of buffalo.

Each of these ways of life was adapted to the land, and to the plants and animals supported by that land. However, Native Americans in the different regions also had some features in common. Indian society was focused on the family and the clan. Those clans belonged to tribes who shared a common language and culture. The tribes in turn were part of language groups.

Native American society recognized certain areas as the territories of different Indian tribes. But land was the source of life, not something that could be bought and sold in parcels. Most Indian peoples believed that their ancestors' spirits were present and could guide them in their lives. These spirits live in the tribe's traditional homeland, which is one reason that their homelands are still sacred to Native Americans.

Exploring and Trading in Louisiana

The Louisiana Purchase

"There is on the globe one single spot," wrote President Thomas Jefferson in 1802, "the possessor of which is our natural . . . enemy." That spot was New Orleans, the point through which any trade goods produced in the Northwest had to flow. At that time, the port of New Orleans belonged to France, which had regained the area from Spain in 1800. Jefferson was determined to win it for the United States. Jefferson told the American minister to France, Robert Livingston, to try to buy New Orleans.

Surprisingly, the French offered instead to sell the whole region of Louisiana. In April 1803, an agreement was made, and the area was sold to the United States at a price of $15 million. Suddenly, the United States had doubled in size.

Even before the United States bought Louisiana, Jefferson wanted to know more about the western lands. In December 1802, he asked Congress for $2,500 to fund an expedition. He put Meriwether Lewis, a former soldier and his personal secretary, in charge. Lewis picked William Clark as his co-commander.

The Lewis and Clark Expedition

Jefferson wanted Lewis and Clark to explore the land and create an accurate map of the course of the Missouri River. He hoped they could find a water route that connected the

"[Louisiana is] a great waste, a wilderness unpeopled with any beings except wolves and wandering Indians. We are to give money of which we have too little for land of which we already have too much."

A Boston newspaper at the time of the Louisiana Purchase

> "In all your [dealings] with the natives, treat them in the most friendly and conciliatory manner which their own conduct will admit."
>
> *President Jefferson's instructions to Meriwether Lewis, July 4, 1803*

Missouri to the Columbia River and thus to the Pacific Ocean. He also wanted them to make note of any plants, animals, and minerals they saw, bring back samples, and try to establish friendly relations with the Native Americans.

Lewis had a special boat built in Pittsburgh, and set off on August 31, 1803. In December, he and Clark reached St. Louis, Missouri, where they spent the winter. On May 14, 1804, Captains Lewis and Clark set out in three boats.

With them were the men they had hired for their "Corps of Discovery." The party included George Drouillard, who was half French Canadian and half Shawnee. Another member was York, Lewis's African American slave. Along to help with the first part of the journey were some French fur traders.

In the fall of 1804, the expedition stopped at the villages of the Mandan Indians, a trading people who lived near what is now Bismarck, South Dakota. Lewis and Clark wintered near the Mandan. In those months, they hired Toussaint Charbonneau and his wife, Sacagawea. She was a Shoshone Indian from the Rocky Mountains, and the explorers hoped she could help them speak to her people when they reached that area. They also thought that traveling with a woman would make them appear more peaceful and less threatening.

In 1807, Patrick Gass, who traveled with Lewis and Clark, published his journal of the expedition. The account was illustrated with engravings of events that took place on the journey, such as this meeting between Lewis and Clark and the Native Americans living in what is now Iowa.

Sacagawea (c.1784–1812 or c.1884)

Sacagawea (whose name means "Bird Woman") was born in a Shoshone village in what is today northern Idaho. Between the ages of 12 and 14, she was kidnapped from her tribe by a war party of the rival Hidatsa tribe. She was given by the Hidatsa to the French trapper Toussaint Charbonneau. In 1804, the pair spent the winter near the Mandan camp at which the Lewis and Clark expedition had stopped. There, Sacagawea gave birth to a child, and she and Charbonneau were asked to join the expedition.

Sacagawea's most important contribution to the expedition was her aid as an interpreter. She also helped as a guide when the travelers neared her people's home in the Rocky Mountains. She gathered food and once saved valuable equipment when a canoe capsized.

Three different records say that Sacagawea died of a fever in 1812. Native American stories say she lived to between 98 and 100 years of age. Research shows that there is some evidence to support this other view. Whatever the story of her death, it is said that more rivers, lakes, and other natural areas are named after her than any other American woman.

The travelers headed up the Missouri River on April 7, 1805. On June 13, they reached the Great Falls of the Missouri: five sets of waterfalls and rapids that stretched 12 miles (19 km) up river. The party spent a month trying to find a way around the rough water. By July 13, they reached Three Forks, where three rivers join to form the Missouri. On August 12, they found the source of the river, high in the Rocky Mountains. They had reached the Continental Divide, which separates westward-flowing rivers from eastward-flowing rivers. And they realized that there was no water route connecting the Missouri to the Columbia.

The whole party crossed the Rocky Mountains and then split into small groups to explore. Lewis and others met three Shoshone women, who took the travelers back to their village. There they were joined by Clark and Sacagawea. After a few minutes, Sacagawea realized that the village chief was her brother and greeted him tearfully. By this time, the travelers

This 1980 sculpture by the western artist Harry Jackson shows Sacagawea, carrying her baby on her back as she did throughout her travels with Lewis and Clark. Without the help of their Native American guides and many other native people along the way, it is doubtful if the expedition would have managed its extraordinary journey through unknown country.

were tired, and many were hurt or ill. Sacagawea's brother gave them horses and guides to continue on west.

On November 7, 1805, they finally saw the Pacific Ocean. Clark recorded the occasion in his journal with the words, "Great joy in camp." The explorers wintered near the shores of the Pacific in a fort they built. The following spring, they set out again for the long journey back.

On September 23, 1806, Lewis and Clark finally returned to St. Louis, having traveled over 7,000 miles (11,300 km). Despite the dangers and the distance, only one member of the party had died, from acute appendicitis. The travelers brought back thousands of pages of detailed notes of what they had seen. They also brought back accurate maps they had made of the land over which they had traveled. In addition to providing important information about the western regions, the Lewis and Clark explorations would later be used to give weight to the United States' claim to the Oregon region.

Other Explorations

To the people of the United States, the West was no longer confined to the region east of the Mississippi River. What had previously been referred to as the West now came to be known as the Old West. Beyond was the Far West, ripe for exploration. The American government sent out other expeditions to explore the Far West. Two journeys were led by army officers, first Zebulon Pike and then Stephen Long.

Pike set out from St. Louis in July 1806. His orders were to find the sources of the Arkansas and Red Rivers. Pike also had orders to find out whatever he could about Spanish strength in the farther Southwest.

Pike and his band of explorers marched through Kansas and southern Nebraska. They picked up the Arkansas River and followed it to its source in present-day Colorado. Along the way, they spied a lone, blue mountain. Pike believed he could use the mountain as a point from which to view and map the surrounding area. It turned out to be farther away than he thought. The explorers became trapped by snow in the high, rocky country leading to the mountain, now known as Pike's Peak. They had to give up the attempt and turn back.

After exploring the Rocky Mountains in Colorado, Pike turned south, reaching a river that fed the Rio Grande. He was in Spanish territory, and soon Pike and his men were captured by Spanish soldiers. They were marched to Santa Fe, now in New Mexico, and then south into Mexico. Though Pike's papers were seized, he made mental notes of everything he saw. Later, he reported in great detail about Spanish troop strength.

Pike's report said the southern Plains lacked the water and trees that would make it suitable for settlement. He did point out, however, the advantages of opening trade with the city

By 1820, white Americans' knowledge of the North American continent had vastly increased. Lewis and Clark had been all the way to the Pacific Ocean. Zebulon Pike had explored the Rockies and down to the Southwest, and Stephen Long had brought back information about the Great Plains.

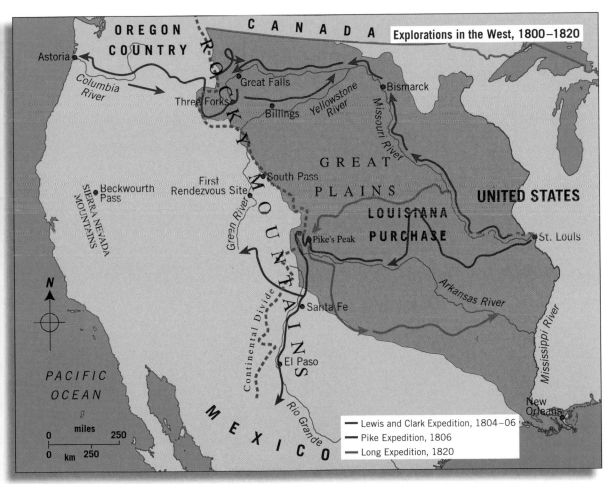

> "I do not hesitate in giving the opinion, that it [the Great Plains region] is almost wholly unfit for cultivation, and of course uninhabitable by a people depending on agriculture."
>
> *Stephen Long, 1823*

Fur trappers in the Rockies often spent months at a time in isolated mountain camps such as the one below. They worked alone or with Native American guides.

of Santa Fe. These two ideas influenced American policy for many years.

Stephen Long traveled some of the same country in his expedition, which began in 1820. Long explored the Arkansas River and its tributaries. He also reached Pike's Peak, and some members of his expedition were the first people known to have climbed that mountain. Long's trip was significant for several reasons. His party had been the first white people to see several plants and animals that lived on the Great Plains, including the coyote. His map greatly increased American knowledge of the geography of the West. Most important, Long confirmed Pike's views that the Great Plains could not be settled. He called the Plains "the Great American Desert." The name stuck for many years to come.

The Fur Trade

In sending out Lewis and Clark, Jefferson wanted to promote trade. His wish quickly came true. The fur trade that had

Manuel Lisa (1772–1820)

Manuel Lisa was born into a Spanish family and raised in New Orleans. In 1798, he moved to St. Louis, hoping to make money in the fur trade. While Spain ruled the Louisiana Territory, he won the exclusive right to trade with the Ozark people. But Lisa could not compete with the Chouteau family, who dominated the fur trade in the area.

Almost as soon as Lewis and Clark returned to St. Louis, Lisa outfitted a fur expedition. He went up the Missouri River to the Yellowstone River and stopped near modern Billings, Montana. There he built a fort and sent his trappers into the wilderness.

Manuel Lisa made so much money on this trip that the Chouteaus were willing to become partners. They formed the St. Louis Missouri Fur Company. William Clark was a partner, too. However, Lisa's company never became a major success. Soon after it started, the War of 1812 broke out, stopping the fur trade. Lisa died in 1820, just before fur trappers opened the Rocky Mountains to the large-scale trade he had imagined.

thrived in the Great Lakes region (the Old Northwest) began to move farther west. As trappers worked the mountain streams of the Rocky Mountains, they learned more about the Far West.

One of the first fur traders to make the move was Manuel Lisa. He recognized that the knowledge gained by Lewis and Clark could be turned into profits. In 1807, Lisa moved up the Missouri River looking for beaver. He was clever enough to hire some veterans of the Lewis and Clark trip to join him. The following spring, Lisa returned to St. Louis with $9,000 worth of beaver pelts. The hunt for furs was on.

Another businessman tried to tap into the fur trade in a different way. In 1811, John Jacob Astor built a trading post, named Astoria, at the mouth of the Columbia River in present-day Oregon. He hoped to obtain furs from other, inland trading posts. Furs would be collected in Astoria, from where they could be shipped around the world. Astor's plan failed when the War of 1812 broke out. However, as the first permanent white settlement in the lower Columbia region, Astoria's existence later helped to validate the American claim to Oregon.

The War of 1812 put a halt to the fur trade because Native American tribes, such as the Mandan, favored the British. It was not until 1822 that trapping began in earnest again. A St. Louis businessman, William H. Ashley, hired a hundred bold, hardy men to head to the Rocky Mountains and find beaver. For the next two decades, the hunt for furs was carried out by these tough adventurers: the mountain men.

The Mountain Men

The mountain men gloried in their freedom in the wild. Their lives were dangerous, as they faced a harsh environment and sometimes fought with Indians. Some of the mountain men were African Americans. Fur trapper James Stephenson pointed out that blacks could "manage [Indians] better than the white men, and with less friction." Even if they were not slaves, blacks still faced prejudice in the East, but in the open lands of the West they had fewer problems.

In 1825, Ashley told the trappers to meet in the summer at a certain spot. The mountain men gathered on the banks of the Green River, near the present-day Wyoming-Utah border. Ashley came from St. Louis to buy their furs and sell them supplies. He returned east after the gathering with beaver pelts valued at $50,000, a huge sum.

The gathering became an annual event known as the rendezvous. The mountain men stayed at the rendezvous for many weeks. After months in isolation,

Jim Beckwourth was one of several African Americans who became mountain men in the 1820s and 1830s. Beckwourth was a former slave who escaped to freedom in the mountains of the West. He married a Native American woman and was adopted into the tribe of the Crow people of the northern Rockies. He later found the pass through the Sierra Nevada Mountains that today bears his name.

The mountain man rendezvous became a huge and festive event. Native American trappers and white and black mountain men came with their families to meet the fur traders who took beaver pelts in exchange for food and other supplies for the coming year.

John Colter (c.1775–1813)

John Colter was a brave, resourceful man who is called by some the first mountain man. Born in Virginia, he was chosen to join the Lewis and Clark expedition. Colter then spent a few years trapping and exploring in the northern Rockies. He became the first white person to set foot in the areas that are now Yellowstone Park and Jackson Hole, Wyoming.

Colter's life was marked by adventure and danger. It is said that he was once captured by a band of Blackfoot Indians. They stripped him naked and told him to run for his life. He outran all who chased him but one, whom he killed. Then Colter dived into a freezing mountain river, where he hid for many hours. After he finally emerged, it took him several days to run about 150 miles (240 km) back to safety.

In 1810, Colter decided to retire from life in the mountains. He traveled 2,000 miles (3,200 km) by canoe to St. Louis, where he related his travels to William Clark, then governor of Louisiana Territory. Clark added Colter's information to his master map of the West. Colter died three years later.

"[The mountain men] engaged in contests of skill at running, jumping, wrestling, shooting with the rifle, and running horses."

Washington Irving, novelist and writer

they enjoyed each other's company, playing games, telling stories, and stocking up for the next winter.

The time of the mountain men was brief. Their efficient work destroyed the beaver population of the region, and by 1840, there were too many trappers and too few beaver. The trade died out, and the mountain men moved to other ventures. However, in their time in the Rocky Mountains, the mountain men helped open up the West to settlers by establishing trails and sharing their knowledge with the early pioneers.

The Mountain Men: Legends and Legacies

Storytelling was a big part of the festivities that took place at the mountain men's annual rendezvous. Many of the stories may have been exaggerated, but they often passed into legend in the West. In one story, Jedidiah Smith had his head ripped apart by the jaws of a grizzly bear, and then asked a companion to stitch his head back together. Jim Bridger is supposed to have carried a three-inch arrowhead in his back for three years.

The mountain men left their mark in other ways. Traveling around mountains, over passes, and along streams, they learned much of the geography of the mountain country. Jedidiah Smith made an important find. In 1823, he and some other mountain men learned from Crow Indians of a way through the Rocky Mountains. The information led them to a pass 20 miles (32 km) wide that came to be known as South Pass, in present-day Wyoming. It was the easiest way to cross the Rockies, and about 20 years later became the main wagon route to Oregon.

Jim Beckwourth, an African American mountain man, also made an important discovery. He found a pass through California's Sierra Nevada mountains. Beckwourth Pass opened the door to California for thousands of gold seekers during the Gold Rush of the late 1840s.

Jim Bridger, who blazed the Bridger Trail through Wyoming's Big Horn Basin, later set up a trading post that served people traveling on the Oregon Trail. Places named after the legendary trappers such as Jim Bridger and John Colter can still be found all over the West today.

The Spanish Southwest and California

What is now an area of the American West was for more than two centuries part of the Spanish empire in the Americas. A huge expanse of land—from Texas to California and up to Utah and Colorado—was claimed by Spain. The Spanish settled some of this land, where they worked and fought with the Native Americans who had lived there for centuries. These settlements were created to protect Spain's North American holdings in Mexico. Three main regions were settled: the area that is now New Mexico and Arizona; Texas; and California.

The Pueblo peoples, such as the Zuñi and the Hopi, were descended from the ancient Anasazi people. Their distinctive style of building can still be seen in the adobe villages of the Southwest. Rooms and houses were built next to and on top of each other, making one large, connected structure.

The Arrival of the Spanish

Spanish interest in the area north of Mexico began in the middle 1500s. In the region that is now Arizona and New Mexico, they found native people living in permanent communities. These people had created irrigation systems to bring water to their fields, where they grew corn, squash, and beans. Using sun-dried clay called adobe, they had built homes that housed many families. The Spanish called each

of these communities a pueblo, meaning town. Native Americans in the region became known as Pueblo Indians.

The Spanish often took what they wanted by force. Worse, the Spanish brought diseases against which the Native Americans had no natural defenses. Smallpox, measles, and other illnesses killed thousands of Indians in the region. This made it easier for the Spanish to take control of the area in later years.

> "[The Pueblos] have a mortal hatred for our holy faith and enmity for the Spanish nation."
>
> *A Spanish officer*

The First Colonies

In August 1598, an expedition led north by Juan de Oñate reached a site near what is now Santa Fe, New Mexico, and Oñate chose to settle there. His group of more than 500 men, women, and children created the first European settlement west of the Mississippi River, named San Juan de los Caballeros.

In the following years, Oñate lost his power over the settlement. But the colony took hold, although it remained small throughout the 1600s. Only about 3,000 people were scattered across present-day New Mexico. Most lived on ranches, using Native Americans who lived nearby as slave labor. In 1609, the governor of the region founded the new capital at Santa Fe.

The Spanish also built missions in New Mexico. These were religious communities set up by Spanish monks who hoped to convert the Indians to Christianity. They tried to force the Native Americans to live like Europeans, teaching them to grow European food such as wheat, peaches, and plums. Pueblo

The Pueblo Revolt

Many Indians in New Mexico bitterly resented the Spanish, and war resulted. In 1680, almost all of the Pueblo Indians rose in revolt. They killed about one-fifth of the Spanish settlers and 21 of the 33 monks. They destroyed all the Spanish buildings, including the churches. The remaining Spanish settlers fled to El Paso with some Indians who remained loyal. The Pueblo Indians kept control of New Mexico for almost ten years, but the Spanish finally returned and regained control in the 1690s.

The Pueblo peoples suffered greatly from disease and Spanish cruelty after the revolt. They never rebelled again. Indeed, they allied with the Spanish against other native peoples, such as the Apache. A measure of peace settled over the region.

peoples began to tend flocks of sheep and herds of cattle and horses, all brought by the Europeans. Their way of life changed dramatically.

The Spanish also moved into modern Arizona, but in even smaller numbers than in New Mexico. Through the 1700s, about a thousand Spanish settlers lived in the southern parts of Arizona. Missions were established, and the Pima Indians who lived in the region slowly adopted some European ways, as the Pueblos had done. Both New Mexico and Arizona remained small outposts of Spanish power, but the cultural influence was lasting.

Building a Barrier

When Oñate first settled New Mexico, Spain was the only European power in North America. As the 1600s and 1700s progressed, that changed. The British now dominated the Atlantic coast. More worrisome to the Spanish were the French, who were moving down the Mississippi River and nearing the Spanish settlements in Mexico. Spain planted missions and built a few forts in what is now Texas to establish a barrier against the French.

The Spanish gave land and other privileges to small groups of people willing to move to Texas. The colony remained quite small, however. Only about 1,850 Spanish settlers lived in Texas in 1763. They developed a distinct way of life based on cattle ranching. These ranchers had good equipment and techniques for tending cattle. Later, their methods would be adopted by American cowboys.

After the French and Indian War ended in 1763, France gave Louisiana to Spain. Again, the Spanish sent colonists, but they were few in number. By 1800, there were fewer Spanish in Louisiana than there were French and Anglos, or English-speaking settlers, in the Southwest.

Clashes in the West

The Spanish now saw the United States as a growing threat to their own position in the Southwest. In 1802, Spain gave

Louisiana back to France. The next year, France sold the vast territory to the United States. The threat that the Spanish feared was right on their doorstep.

Meanwhile, the Spanish and Native Americans of Texas often fought. The Comanche and the Apache raided ranches and settlements to take livestock and guns. The Spanish fought back, sometimes taking Indian children as captives and making them slaves. That angered the Native Americans more and provoked new attacks.

While they ruled Louisiana, the Spanish noticed that the French maintained generally good relations with Native Americans through trade. In the late 1700s, a Spanish official named Bernardo de Gálvez suggested a new approach to Indian relations. Instead of fighting with Native Americans, they should try trading with them. He hoped, too, that the Indians would adopt European ways of life.

The main thrust of Gálvez's plan worked. Native Americans were now given access to European goods they wanted, particularly guns and horses. They generally stopped raiding, and peace more or less prevailed in Texas for several decades. Meanwhile, the Spanish had to respond to another threat, in the region that is now California.

To the Pacific Coast

In the 1530s and 1540s, Spanish explorers had sailed along the coast of present-day California as far north as what is now Oregon. The Spanish never made any attempts to settle the land, but they regarded it as theirs. In the 1700s, Spain worried about moves by other European nations onto this land. The British had long claimed this region themselves. And in 1759, a new player appeared on the scene. Russians set up trading posts along the Pacific coast, including one just north of San Francisco.

José de Gálvez—Bernardo's uncle, and a man with great power—decided to counter the Russian threat. In 1769, he recruited a Franciscan monk, Junipero Serra, and the Spanish military to build missions and forts in California. The

The California Missions

The missions in California were run by Roman Catholic monks called Franciscans, who followed the teachings of St. Francis of Assisi. They dedicated their lives to helping the poor and suffering, and to teaching their religion. They also had to live in poverty themselves.

The early California missions were founded by Father Junipero Serra, who arrived in California in 1769. The missions were actually built by Native Americans recruited by the Franciscans who hoped to convert them to Christianity and use them as agricultural laborers. Discipline and religion were enforced by the monks with the help of Spanish soldiers who lived in barracks at the missions or in nearby forts.

By the early 1820s, the Franciscans had built a string of 21 missions up the coast to San Francisco. The missions were far more successful than those in the other Spanish colonies. Some did better than others, depending on the fertility of their land and the attitudes of local tribes.

At their height, the missions housed more than 20,000 Native Americans. The men's work consisted mostly of farming, ranching, and leather work. Women made candles and soap, wove materials, and tended gardens, vineyards, and orchards.

In the 1820s and 1830s, the missions were broken up. Mexico, which had won its independence from Spain, wanted to reduce the power of the Catholic Church.

Part of a 1930s mural showing Indians laboring in a California mission.

presence of the settlements had the desired effect, and the Russian trading posts never grew very large.

As elsewhere, however, the coming of the Spanish to California was devastating to Native Americans. About 300,000 Indians lived in California in 1769. By 1821, the numbers may have been half that. Diseases from white settlers caused most of the deaths.

The original hunting and gathering culture of the Native Americans had been destroyed when they had been forced into farming at the missions. When the mission system ended after Mexican independence in 1821, the Native Americans could not return to their old life, but now they did not have the land or resources to farm either.

Spanish Society

Spanish settlers in California, as in the Southwest, were few. The biggest single group was soldiers. Some finished their army service and then received grants of land, which they used to establish ranches.

Spanish society in these frontier regions had a special character. In Mexico, the Spanish lived on huge estates with land worked by Indian slaves. That did not happen in the northern regions. In theory, slavery was illegal, although wealthy settlers had unpaid workers called servants who were, really, slaves. More important, though, was the dry, harsh land of the Southwest. It was not suited to large estates, and the small landowners there were more likely to work in the fields themselves.

Trade Opens Up

Trade was an important part of the economy in the Spanish colonies. California missions produced wheat and leather. In New Mexico, herds of sheep provided wool, and Texas had cattle and horses. These goods were all shipped south to other Spanish regions. Spain had strict rules banning its colonies from trading with Americans or other powers. They wanted to keep profits within the Spanish empire.

That situation changed in 1821, when Mexico won its independence from Spain. The region from Texas to California was no longer part of the Spanish empire. Now, these areas were provinces of Mexico. And the Mexicans welcomed trade with the United States.

In 1821, the American trader William Becknell left Missouri carrying goods to Santa Fe. His trip brought profits, and the route he took became the Santa Fe Trail. The route remained in use for more than two decades, as trade thrived. Native Americans were a danger to those who traveled alone, so traders took to joining together in caravans. They brought manufactured goods, which they traded in Santa Fe for gold, silver, and furs.

Settlers in Texas

Before Mexican independence, the colonies in what is now Texas still had few settlers. The Comanches began raiding again. The damage the Indians caused seemed worse to the Spanish than the threat from Anglos. Spanish officials decided to invite Anglos to settle in the region. They offered grants of land to people known as *empresarios*, who promised to bring settlers. The more settlers, they brought, the more land the *empresarios* received. But after Mexico won its independence from Spain, it was not clear if the new government would recognize the Spanish land grants.

Stephen Austin was the son of a former lead miner, Moses Austin, who had been awarded a land grant by the Spanish.

By 1821, the old Spanish town of Santa Fe, founded in 1609, had long been the center of commerce for Spanish traders in New Mexico. When Mexico became independent from Spain, American traders were eager to bring their goods from the east to Santa Fe, where they could make good profits. Within a few years of Becknell's first journey in 1821, many wagon trains were making their way along the Santa Fe Trail to the prosperous capital of New Mexico.

Stephen Fuller Austin (1793–1836)

Austin was born on the southwestern frontier of Virginia. His father, Moses Austin, had moved there from his native Connecticut to operate a lead mine. When Stephen was five, the family moved again, this time to Missouri.

Young Austin's early years prepared him well for his later life. Missouri was a mixed society, with people of French, Spanish, and American descent. This readied him for the different cultures of Texas. He also learned many different skills in various jobs.

Stephen Austin led the first large group of settlers into Texas in 1822. He won influence with and respect from the leaders in Mexico and the United States. But tensions between the Anglos in Texas and the Mexican government grew. In 1833, a group of Texans met and demanded that Texas be separated from Mexico and become independent. Austin traveled to Mexico City to push the demand. While he was there, he was arrested and held for a year and a half. When he returned to Texas, the war for Texan independence was about to break out. He helped the effort by traveling to the United States to try and raise funds and support.

Austin served as the secretary of state to the Republic of Texas until his death. He had set out to "pave the way for civilization and lay the foundation for lasting . . . wealth, morality, and happiness" in Texas. Called the "Father of Texas," he was the most important and powerful leader in the area for many years. The state capital of Texas is named for him.

When his father died suddenly, Stephen Austin convinced Mexican officials to continue the grant. He brought in settlers and became a leader of the Anglos in Texas.

Austin and others sent agents to the United States to praise the benefits of Texas. But American settlers would have to follow certain rules. They had to promise to learn Spanish and join the Catholic Church, and they had to obey Mexican laws. These promises proved troublesome. Many of the settlers who came to Texas had left homes in the South. They came with slaves, hoping to find land on which to grow cotton. But the Mexican constitution banned slavery.

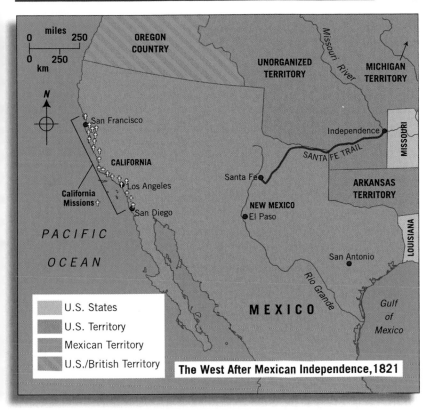

The West After Mexican Independence, 1821

Map legend:
- U.S. States
- U.S. Territory
- Mexican Territory
- U.S./British Territory

After 1821, the Southwest and California were still largely inhabited by Hispanics and Native Americans. But trails from the East to the West had opened up, and Anglos dominated in Texas by the 1830s. They were soon to set their sights on other areas of the West.

Anglo-Mexican Conflict

Relations between the Anglo settlers and the Mexican government were often poor. Over time, the government grew alarmed at the growing numbers of Anglos. In 1830, Mexico banned further settlement by Americans, but it was too late.

Not only in Texas but elsewhere in the Southwest, Anglos and Hispanic settlers often had bad relations. Mistrust and misunderstanding appeared on both sides. José María Sánchez was sent by the Mexican government to survey the border between Texas and Mexico. Objecting to the Anglos' practice of slavery, he called them "lazy people of vicious character." Richard Henry Dana—a New Englander who visited Mexican California—had a similar view of the Hispanics there. "Idle, thriftless people," he called them. However, conflict was not always the rule. Several towns had prominent merchants who had been born in the United States, moved to California, and married Hispanic women.

In Texas, Austin tried to maintain smooth relations with both Hispanic settlers and the Mexican government. But tension was rising. More than 30,000 Anglos lived in Texas by 1835, far more than the few thousand Hispanics. Their main loyalty was not to the government in Mexico City, but to the United States. That nation would soon hear a loud, public clamor for expansion. And the northern provinces of Mexico would be swept up in the result.

The Russians and Alaska

Although its colonies along the Pacific coast were overcome by a strong Spanish presence, Russia still had a foothold in North America. In 1784, the Russian government had sent settlers to build the first white colony in Alaska, on Kodiak Island. Alaska was already inhabited by Native Americans: Inuit, Aleut, Athabascan, Tlingit, and Haida peoples all lived in the region.

The Russians were interested in trapping animals, especially seals, for fur. The Russian-American Company developed the area and established a number of further settlements. Russians farmed, mined for coal, and built foundries for producing iron.

In the early 1800s, British and Americans trappers also worked in Alaska. Treaties in the 1820s set boundaries and trading rights. But conflicts with Britain led the Russian government to withdraw its support of the Russian-American Company. Alaska had become a burden, and the Russians offered to sell the territory to the United States.

William Seward, U.S. secretary of the interior, believed Alaska was rich in resources and encouraged the government to add the vast area to the United States' possessions. Many Americans felt the region was useless to them, and named it "Seward's Folly." After much argument and an extremely close vote, Congress approved the purchase of Alaska on April 9, 1867. The price was $7,200,000, or two cents an acre. The United States had expanded even farther west.

4

Manifest Destiny

In 1845, the magazine editor John L. O'Sullivan gave a name to a movement. The American people had a "manifest destiny to overspread the continent." That destiny came from God, and no other people could stop it. O'Sullivan argued that the United States had a natural right to the entire North American continent. O'Sullivan and others even saw this right to expand as Americans' duty. They were to bring western civilization and democracy from the Atlantic to the Pacific.

There were problems with the United States fulfilling this destiny, however. First, thousands of Native Americans lived throughout North America. Another problem was that the Oregon Country was claimed by both the United States and Great Britain. This large territory included present-day Oregon, Washington, and Idaho as well as the far western parts of Canada. And the vast region from California to Texas and north to Utah and Colorado belonged to Mexico. All this would have to change if Americans were to control the continent.

> "It [the right of the United States to expand] is a right such as that of the tree to the space of air and earth suitable for the full expansion of its principle and destiny of growth."
>
> *John L. O'Sullivan, editor,* The United States Magazine and Democratic Review, *1845*

Rebellion in Texas

Tensions between Anglos in Texas and the Mexican government increased in the 1830s. Then a change in Mexican politics caused a revolution in Texas. In 1833, General Antonio Lopez de Santa Anna made himself the ruler of Mexico. Santa Anna believed in strong central power. Late in 1835, he declared a new constitution that put the national government firmly in charge.

Many Texans resented this move. On December 20, 1835, a group of Texans met and declared their wish to become independent from what they called Santa Anna's illegal

For 12 days, 187 men in the Alamo fought off the Mexican army outside. But they did not stand a chance against Santa Anna's 3,000 soldiers.

"I shall never surrender or retreat. . . . I am determined to sustain myself as long as possible and die like a soldier who never forgets what is due to his own honor or that of his country."

Colonel William Travis, the Alamo, 1836

government. The rebels named Sam Houston, formerly governor of Tennessee, as their army's commander. Although most of the rebels were Anglos, there were some Hispanics as well.

The Texans began to clash with Mexican government forces. Santa Anna gathered an army and marched to Texas. The Texas rebels seized several Mexican forts. In February 1836, they took over the Alamo in San Antonio, but they were overcome by a huge Mexican force. Soon after, the Mexicans captured the garrison in the town of Goliad, where, on March 27, they put to death more than 300 Texas rebels.

The Lone Star Republic

Houston's army began falling back, and Santa Anna's larger force pursued. In April 1836, at San Jacinto near what is now Houston, the Texans stopped and launched a surprise attack. They yelled "Remember the Alamo! Remember Goliad!" as they charged into battle. In just 18 minutes, they defeated the Mexican army and captured Santa Anna. Houston forced him to surrender and recognize the independence of Texas.

In September 1836, Houston was elected the first president of the Republic of Texas. At the same time, Texans expressed their wish for the United States to annex Texas.

However, the United States was increasingly torn by the debate over the spread of slavery. Many in the North would not accept Texas as a new state because slavery existed there. But in the South, people were growing angry at what they saw as attempts to limit slavery. For a while, Texas remained an independent country. It was also a growing country, as thousands of Americans poured into the new republic.

The Alamo

The Alamo in San Antonio was originally a Spanish mission. Against the orders of General Houston, Texas rebels led by William B. Travis and James Bowie took over the building and refused to surrender to the Mexican army.

Some Americans, spurred by the idea of people fighting for their rights, had hurried to Texas. The frontiersman Davy Crockett led a small group of fighters from Tennessee for that reason. They brought the defenders at the Alamo up to 187 men. When Santa Anna's 3,000 soldiers arrived, Colonel Travis sent a message from inside the Alamo "to the people of Texas and all the Americans in the World." In it, he declared his men's will to fight.

On March 6, 1836, after 12 days of fighting, the Alamo fell to the attackers. The 187 defenders—the Texans and their American allies—were all killed, and Santa Anna ordered their bodies to be piled up and burned.

Oregon Fever

Meanwhile in the 1830s, another area was becoming the object of United States expansion. American missionaries began to enter Oregon Country, hoping to convert the Native Americans there to Christianity. They sent back glowing reports of what they found. By 1838, people in Lynn, Massachusetts, had created an Oregon Emigration Society.

The government stepped in next. Thomas Hart Benton, a senator from Missouri, believed strongly in American expansion. In 1842 and 1843, his son-in-law John Charles Frémont, also a believer in Manifest Destiny, was put in charge of two expeditions to find a wagon route to Oregon Country. Frémont's wife, Jessie Benton, wrote romantic reports of his journeys, gaining him fame as "The Pathfinder." These reports raised more excitement about Oregon.

Soon, many people were taking the path west on the Oregon Trail. The "Great Migration" had begun. In 1843, about 1,000 people made the trip. The next year, it was about 1,400. More than 3,000 people reached Oregon in 1845. A decision was needed to settle the status of Oregon. Britain,

"The Oregon fever is raging in almost every part of the Union. Companies are forming . . . and will make a pretty formidable army. This, if nothing else, will compel Congress to act upon the matter."

An Iowa newspaper on the question of Oregon's status

The Oregon Trail

The Oregon Trail began in Independence, Missouri, and stretched to the Pacific Ocean. It ran about 2,000 miles (3,200 km) and took from 150 to 180 days to travel. Families piled themselves and their goods in covered wagons that weighed from 3,000 to 7,000 pounds (1,360 to 3,200 kg). Some wagons were so heavy that 10 to 12 horses, mules, or oxen were needed to pull them. People gathered into groups, called wagon trains, and hired captains to guide them over the long trail.

The captains told families to leave behind furniture, which added weight and slowed the trip. Even then, the trail was often littered with goods that families had to leave along the way. The captains also provided lists of food to bring and set a steady pace so the trains would reach water and good grazing for the animals at noon and at the end of each day. With good weather and even ground, a wagon train could cover 15 to 20 miles (24 to 32 km) a day.

The trains rarely had trouble with Native Americans. Occasionally there were fights, but Indians often acted as guides and tracked down livestock that strayed from the wagon trains. They supplied the travelers with food and traded horses when the travelers lost animals to disease or injury.

Sioux Indians sit on the bank of the Platte River in what is now Nebraska, while a wagon train heading west on the Oregon Trail makes its way through the water.

like the United States, still claimed the land. James Knox Polk ran for president in 1844, promising to win all of the Oregon Country up to the southern border of Alaska. Polk won the election, and when Britain refused his demand for the land, there was talk of possible war.

Soon, Polk and the British found a compromise. They agreed on a border, along the 49th parallel, that was farther north than the British wanted and farther south than Polk had claimed. In June 1846, the Senate approved the Oregon Treaty. Oregon below the 49th parallel was firmly in the United States.

Narcissa Prentiss Whitman (1808–1847)

Narcissa Prentiss Whitman and her husband Marcus Whitman, a doctor, set out for Oregon from New York after listening to a minister named Samuel Parker. Parker spoke of the great need for missionaries to bring Christianity to the Native Americans living in Oregon Country.

In 1836, Narcissa Whitman and Eliza Spalding, who also made the trip with her clergyman husband, became the first white women to travel the Oregon Trail. The Whitmans and Spaldings settled in the Walla Walla Valley, in what is now Washington State.

The Whitmans' mission was among the Cayuse tribe. They taught the Cayuse about farming and raising cattle, but did not succeed in bringing the native people to Christianity. Though full of religious spirit, Narcissa Whitman was poorly suited to missionary life. She missed her family and suffered tragedy when her only daughter drowned. Over time, she fell victim to depression.

Gradually, the Whitmans spent less and less time on missionary work among the Cayuse. They devoted more attention to the white settlers, although when measles broke out in 1847, they tried to care for the Cayuse people. But the Cayuse had no immunity to the disease and many of their children died. Because the white settlers' children recovered more often, the Indians suspected the Whitmans of poisoning native children when treating them. On November 29, a group of Cayuse killed Narcissa Whitman, her husband, and 12 others.

The Mexican War

While the Oregon question was being settled, the United States was looking toward Mexican lands once again. In 1845, John Tyler, the president before Polk, had signed a bill that brought Texas into the Union. Polk was eager to gain even more lands, and wanted to win the northern provinces of Mexico for the United States.

The annexation of Texas deeply angered the Mexican government. So did the American claim that the Rio Grande formed the border between Mexico and the United States. Mexico said the border was farther north, on the Nueces River.

In 1845, Polk sent a diplomat to try to buy California and settle the Texas boundary issue. When the diplomat was not even received by the Mexican government, Polk sent troops into the disputed area in Texas. Mexican soldiers attacked them, and Polk asked Congress to declare war on Mexico. Congress did so on May 13, 1846.

The Battle of Buena Vista was fought in February 1847, in the middle of the Mexican War. It was a great victory for the Americans, even though the Mexican forces greatly outnumbered theirs. The American army under General Zachary Taylor defeated each advance on its camp in northern Mexico, and fought fiercely until the Mexicans were forced to retreat south.

American forces took the northern Mexican city of Monterrey in September 1846. In December, the United States seized the capital of New Mexico, and then part of the army moved on to California. There, Anglo settlers proclaimed an independent "Bear Flag Republic." Their revolt was aided by troops led by John Charles Frémont, who marched down from Oregon, and by American naval forces.

In March 1847, another huge naval force under General Winfield Scott, the United States Army's supreme commander, sailed south through the Gulf of Mexico to Vera Cruz. The town was quickly captured, and the Americans moved west toward Mexico City. After several months and some very bloody battles along the way, the Americans occupied Mexico City in September 1847.

The Treaty of Guadalupe Hidalgo

In March 1848, Mexico and the United States agreed to the Treaty of Guadalupe Hidalgo. The treaty gave the United States the areas that are now California, Nevada, and Utah, almost all of Arizona and New Mexico, and part of Colorado. It also set the U.S.-Mexican border at the Rio Grande. In return, the United States paid Mexico $15 million. In 1853, the United States bought more land from Mexico. Known as the Gadsden Purchase, it included the southern parts of Arizona and New Mexico.

The change in ownership had a devastating impact on the Hispanics who lived in these regions. They had to recognize new laws and adapt to a new language. Many lost their livelihoods because the land that had been granted to them when the area was settled under Spanish rule was taken away.

The United States government had promised to protect the rights of Hispanic landowners. But the boundaries of their land were often unclear, and the process of ruling on all their cases took years. In the meantime, Anglos often abused the system and settled on the land illegally. Many Hispanics, including Pío de Jesus Pico, California's last governor under Mexican rule, never regained their land.

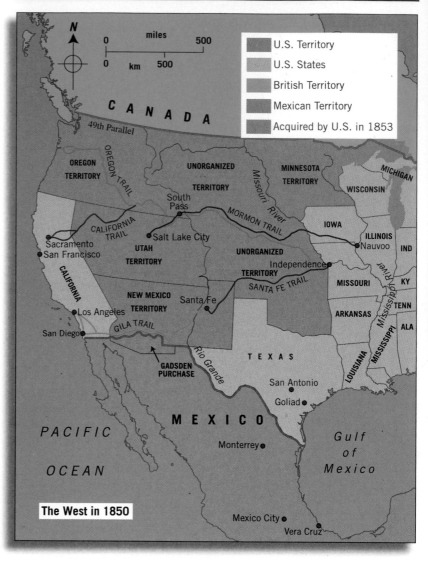

The West in 1850

Between 1845 and 1850, the United States had almost completed its expansion across the North American continent. The Oregon Territory had been formally acquired in 1846. Texas was now a state in the Union. Mexico had ceded huge areas of the West to the United States in 1848. California and all the land to the east of it were now American territory. The Gadsden Purchase of 1853 later added the final piece of the jigsaw.

"Gold!"

The treaty ending the Mexican War was signed on February 2, 1848. Just days before, a major discovery had taken place in California. A crew of workers building a sawmill near Sacramento found gold. It was on the land of Johann August Sutter, a German settler.

Sutter hoped to keep the find a secret. He feared it would be bad for his business. But one of the workers used a flake of gold to buy a drink, and word spread. Sutter was right: His

The California gold prospectors, like these men near Spanish Flats in 1852, used a wooden trough called a "long tom" in their search for gold. It worked like a sieve: The prospectors ran water through gravel and rocks to wash away sand and dirt, hoping to be left with nuggets of gold. Only the lucky few were successful.

land was soon torn up by those, including his own workers, who hoped to find gold.

When word of gold spread beyond California, people were electrified. By 1849, more than 100,000 people had come to the area. The first arrivals were called "forty-niners," named after the year they reached California. The area's population had been only 14,000 before the discovery of gold. By 1852, California held more than 250,000 people.

The Prospectors

These people came from all over the world. Americans came from the Northeast and the South. Some people who had just come west on the Oregon Trail abandoned their farms to look for gold. Others came from Europe and from South America. About 6,000 traveled north from Mexico. By 1852, more than 20,000 Chinese had come to the land they called "Gold Mountain."

In 1848, there were about 800 people living in San Francisco. By 1850, when this photograph was taken, it was a city with 25,000 inhabitants. Two years before, the busy roadway of Montgomery Street, bustling with people, wagons, and cable cars, had been the empty shoreline of Yerba Buena Cove. The cove was completely filled in during the Gold Rush to create more land.

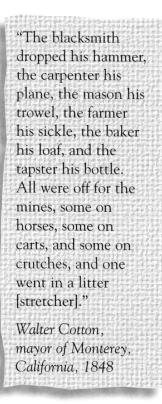

"The blacksmith dropped his hammer, the carpenter his plane, the mason his trowel, the farmer his sickle, the baker his loaf, and the tapster his bottle. All were off for the mines, some on horses, some on carts, and some on crutches, and one went in a litter [stretcher]."

Walter Cotton, mayor of Monterey, California, 1848

The gold seekers, or prospectors, knew that they needed order, and agreed to some basic rules. Claims were respected, and people were encouraged not to claim more land than they could work. Prospectors banned slavery, fearing that groups of enslaved workers could work more land than individuals working alone.

But slaves did come, accompanying their owners. Biddy Mason made the entire trip from Mississippi walking behind the wagons of her master. She later won her freedom, settled in Los Angeles, and became a wealthy property owner. Altogether a few thousand African Americans came to find gold, including free blacks looking to make their fortunes.

California Booms

At first, prospectors could find gold dust and nuggets carried by the water of mountain streams. As time went on, this easy gold became scarce. To obtain gold, prospectors had to dig into mountains. This large-scale gold mining required big companies with large sums of money. But the hopeful thousands kept pouring into California as late as 1859.

San Francisco, the port nearest the gold fields, became a boom town. Soon new towns sprang up. Merchants moved in, supplying the food, equipment, and other supplies the prospectors needed.

California's population explosion changed it from a quiet Hispanic farming and ranching society. It was now a bustling business center with people from many different cultures. Thousands of Americans also came to farm, following the Oregon Trail and then turning south. American settlers dominated the region, and in September 1850, California was admitted to the Union as a state.

Deseret

The 1840s saw a large migration to one other area of the Far West. Thousands of people moved to what is now Utah. This migration was unique, because these thousands of settlers were members of one religion.

Mormons are those who belong to the Church of Jesus Christ of the Latter-Day Saints. In 1844, non-Mormons in Illinois had turned against the Mormons living there. The Mormon leader Joseph Smith was killed and other Mormons determined it was time to move.

The new Mormon leader was Brigham Young. He had seen a report by Frémont that the land around the Great Salt Lake was a good place to settle. (This region, now in the state of Utah,

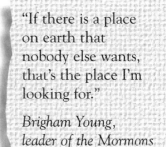

"If there is a place on earth that nobody else wants, that's the place I'm looking for."

Brigham Young, leader of the Mormons

Many travelers on the Mormon Trail, and other trails to the West, were too poor to have wagons and horses. Instead, they piled their possessions into handcarts that they pushed across the plains and mountains between Illinois and Utah.

was still Mexican territory at the time.) In February 1846, Young led 1,800 Mormons west. Hundreds more followed behind. After a terrible winter, when about 600 people died, they reached the Great Salt Lake in summer 1847.

In 1848, after the Mexican War ended, the Utah region became part of the United States. The Mormons asked to join the Union as the state of Deseret, but Congress would not agree. In 1850, the Utah Territory was created, with Young as its governor. The Mormons ran their land as they wished.

In 1857, President James Buchanan named a non-Mormon as the new governor of Utah. When the Mormons refused to recognize him, Buchanan sent army troops to force the issue. The so-called Mormon War ended without fighting. The Mormons accepted the governor appointed by the U.S. government, but Brigham Young actually ruled the territory.

The Mormons

Joseph Smith of New York founded the Mormon religion in 1830 when he published The Book of Mormon. This book, he said, was a translation of secret golden tablets that had been written by an angel.

The Mormon faith grew gradually, viewed with mistrust and suspicion by others. The Mormons eventually chose to settle in Utah because it had few inhabitants. Controversy arose in 1852, when Brigham Young declared publicly what had previously been rumored. The Mormons, he said, believed in polygamy, which meant that a man could have more than one wife at the same time. Utah did not became a state until 1896, after Mormons declared the practice illegal.

Today there are almost 8 million Mormons. Most live in the United States. Each year, many thousands of young Mormons begin two years of missionary work. They travel in the United States and abroad to preach their faith.

In 1997, Mormons celebrated the 150th anniversary of the original Mormon migration of 1846 to 1847. About 8,000 Mormons took part in a re-creation of the wagon trip west. For part of the trip, they moved parallel to the original wagon train route, where the land still shows the ruts made by the old wagon wheels.

5

Linking East and West

As more and more people began to settle the West, new problems arose. Vast stretches of land had to be crossed to move people, goods, or information from the Atlantic coast to the Pacific. In the middle of the 1800s, business people launched several different enterprises to solve this problem. New technology played an important role. So did the federal government, providing tax breaks, land, and loans to help new enterprises.

New Mail Routes to the West

In the late 1840s and early 1850s, there were two ways of getting mail to California. The sea route, crossing Central America overland at Nicaragua or Panama and then heading north, took 30 days. The overland journey was even worse: It took months.

Nor did the shipments of mail run frequently. One company hauled mail from Independence, Missouri, to Salt Lake City, and from there to San Francisco. But it only ran once a month. In 1856, a petition signed by 75,000 Californians asked the government to start an overland mail route to the coast. The government agreed to cover part of the costs of a business willing to undertake the job. But the company had to deliver the mail from the Mississippi River to California within 25 days. The contract was won by John Butterfield, who had founded the American Express Company, and William C. Fargo.

Butterfield built a series of stations along a southern route. The route went from St. Louis to Fort Smith, Arkansas,

Stagecoaches delivered the mail, but they also carried people across the continent. On the western trails, such as this one through the Sierra Nevada Mountains, stagecoaches crowded with passengers soon added to the traffic.

"It [the Overland Express] is a glorious triumph for civilization and the Union."

President James Buchanan in a telegram to John Butterfield, 1858

across Texas to El Paso and then on to Yuma, Arizona, and Los Angeles before finally turning north for San Francisco. (See map on page 57.) Butterfield invested the huge sum of $1 million. He bought stagecoaches made in Concord, New Hampshire, and stocked his stations with horses and mules to pull the coaches. On September 16, 1858, Butterfield himself loaded the mail onto the first coach. Twenty-four days later, on October 10, the Overland Express clattered into San Francisco.

Despite the legends of Hollywood movies, the Overland Express was rarely attacked by robbers. The company made a policy of not carrying gold or silver to try to discourage such problems. And there is only one recorded instance of a Native American attack on an Overland Express coach.

The government was happy with the reliability of the service. It began to offer new mail routes. Butterfield and Fargo joined with Henry Wells in 1852 to create Wells, Fargo and Company. They came to dominate the mail and shipping business in California.

The Pony Express

One company, Russell, Majors, and Waddell, started a famous mail service to compete with Wells, Fargo. The Pony Express relied on a chain of single riders on fast horses.

Each rider would carry the mail for 75 to 125 miles (120 to 200 km), changing to a fresh horse at stations set 10 to 15 miles (16 to 24 km) apart. When the rider completed his leg of the trip, he would gallop into a station and throw the mail pouch to a new rider, who immediately set out on his own journey. The riders rode night and day, regardless of the weather. Eighty riders were on the road at the same time, half of them traveling west and half going east.

The Pony Express was the fastest way to get mail across the continent. The 1,900-mile (3,000-km) journey from St. Joseph, Missouri, to Sacramento took ten days. The riders became heroes, and boys dreamed of the chance to become one of them. But the dream didn't last long. The Pony Express ran only from April 1860 to October 1861. It was overtaken by new technology: the telegraph.

A poster advertising the Pony Express mail service.

The Telegraph

All the mail routes had competition, however, in the form of the telegraph. The first telegraph line had been laid in the East in 1844. By 1852, there were 15,000 miles (24,000 km) of telegraph lines, but none west of the Mississippi. In 1861, the first telegraph pole was stuck in the ground to begin the western system. Workers on the lines moved east from California and west from the Mississippi. On October 24, 1861, the lines were joined, at Fort Bridger in Utah Territory, and messages could flash across the country almost instantly.

A Pony Express rider passes men building telegraph lines, but the telegraph service would soon outstrip the mail service. The telegraph wires took minutes instead of days to deliver messages from coast to coast.

Western Union, the company that ran the telegraph, benefited from government generosity. When the Civil War broke out in 1861, the government had to string 14,000 miles (22,500 km) of telegraph wire for military use. At the end of the war, it simply gave the lines to Western Union.

The Transcontinental Railroad

The biggest change to travel and transportation came with the railroad. As early as 1845, California merchant Asa Whitney urged Congress to build a railroad linking East to West. Two problems blocked any action. First, huge amounts of money were needed to fund the effort. Second, no one could agree on the route that the tracks should follow. Supporters in both North and South wanted trains to roll through their own region. Many people, especially Californians, were unhappy over the lack of action.

The stalemate ended with the onset of the Civil War. North and South were at war, and the Southerners were gone from Congress. Congress wanted to keep California in the

Union, and it approved the building of one railroad from San Francisco to the east and another from Kansas to the west. The government gave generous grants of land and loans to the two railroad companies, the Central Pacific and the Union Pacific.

The Railroad Workers

The Central Pacific railroad grew eastward from California. In 1865, the company hired 50 Chinese laborers to work on the line. When they proved excellent workers, the company hired more. Eventually, more than 15,000 Chinese toiled on the railroad, about 90 percent of the entire workforce of the Central Pacific.

Their work was hard. They had to cut trees, carry heavy rails, and blast tunnels in the mountains. The bosses constantly pressured them to work harder and faster. In the winter of 1866, they were told to build over the passes of the Sierra Nevada Mountains of California. Huge drifts of snow towered 60 feet (18 m) high. The workers cut tunnels in the snow, and when the drifts collapsed, they froze or suffocated to death. Avalanches carried others down the mountains. Hundreds died that winter, and hundreds more during the five years of work.

Despite the dangers, the Chinese workers were paid much less than the white workers received. They worked six days a week, 12 hours a day. In the spring of 1867, about 5,000 Chinese railroad workers went on strike for more money and an eight-hour work day. The railroad company cut off all food to the striking workers. Within a week, the half-starved Chinese ended their strike.

In the meantime, the Union Pacific built the track from the Missouri River (at Omaha in present-day Nebraska) toward the West. The crews working on this railroad were largely Irish. Others were former Confederate soldiers and African Americans now freed from slavery. These workers had to watch for attacks by Sioux and Comanche Indians and stampedes by huge herds of buffalo. But they could work faster than the Central Pacific workers because they had better terrain with no mountains. They laid 250 miles (400 km) of track in the first six months and 500 miles (800 km) in 1866 and 1867.

Many Chinese people came to California during the Gold Rush. Thousands of them later found work building railroads in the West.

The Chinese workers [on the railroad] were "a great army laying siege to Nature in her strongest citadel."

Albert P. Richardson, Beyond the Mississippi, *1867*

Work began in earnest when the Civil War ended. The Central Pacific and the Union Pacific began a race to lay as much track as possible. The more track a company laid, the larger its land grants and loans. Finally, on May 10, 1869, the great enterprise was completed. The two lines met at Promontory Point, Utah, near the Great Salt Lake. Company leaders and government officials came from both directions.

The workers hammered down all but the last spike to connect a rail to a wooden tie. That was saved for the officials. They took turns using a silver hammer to hit a golden spike. When the spike was finally driven, telegraphs sent the news across the nation: "It is done."

Soon, other railroads spanned the country. The Atchison, Topeka, and Santa Fe stretched from Kansas to Colorado and New Mexico. The Southern Pacific connected New Orleans, Tucson, and Los Angeles. The Northern Pacific linked St. Paul, Minnesota, to Portland, Oregon. The Great Northern stretched from St. Paul, Minnesota, all the way to Seattle, Washington.

With the railroads came cities. From Houston and Denver to Los Angeles and Spokane, the cities grew because they were now important rail centers. Many Pacific coast ports thrived. They were now able to take goods from the nation's interior and ship them to cities in Asia and Latin America.

Industries Boom

The growth of cities created demand for another product: lumber. In 1850, during the Gold Rush, lumbermen moved into the forests of the Northwest. They brought the lumber

By 1900, many new railroads crossed the continent, carrying goods and passengers from east to west and back. Along the routes, cities grew and trade flourished.

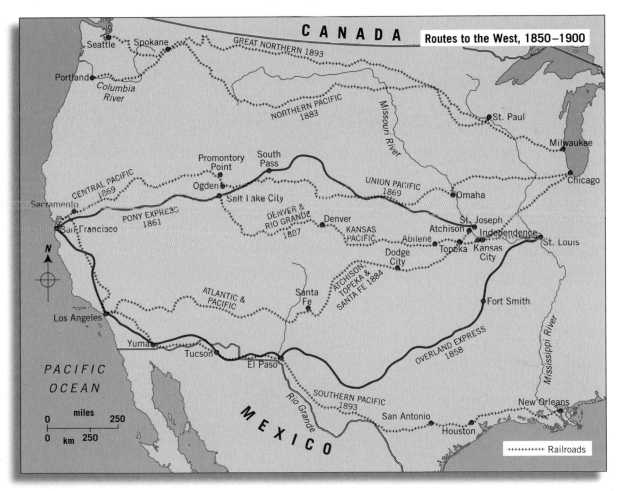

Routes to the West, 1850–1900

down to booming San Francisco. Soon, more and more wood was being harvested.

Other companies followed, hoping to use the vast forests of the Northwest. They hired experienced lumbermen from New England and the Great Lakes region. Razor sharp saws and falling trees made lumbering a very dangerous industry. Many workers were killed or lost limbs in accidents. But they kept cutting, and the companies used railroads to ship lumber in all directions.

At the same time, another industry was expanding. Mining grew as new mineral strikes created gold and silver rushes across the West. None created the huge flow of people that California's Gold Rush had. But the new mines generated great sums of money. The biggest strike was the Comstock Lode, found in about 1857 on the eastern slope of the Sierra Nevada Mountains. The Comstock Lode eventually produced more than $300 million worth of silver and gold.

Gold strikes happened elsewhere. In 1858, hopeful miners streamed to Colorado for gold and silver. In 1863, two areas in Montana yielded more than $46 million worth of gold.

Towns sprang up and flourished in mining areas. Denver became a major city, where Barney Ford and Henry Wagoner, two African Americans, built a string of businesses providing services and supplies to miners and travelers. But often, when the precious metals were all gone, the miners moved on. Soon, the merchants who relied on the miners' business left as well, leaving ghost towns behind them.

In Nevada City, a ghost town in Montana, the Star Bakery and the Emporium that once served miners have stood empty since the 1800s. The population of mining towns in the West could grow to thousands in a matter of months and just as quickly disappear altogether. In most ghost towns, only a few foundations remain to show what was once there. In a few cases, however, a small number of people stayed on, and the abandoned buildings were preserved and later restored.

Chinese Americans

During the Gold Rush of the 1850s, thousands of Chinese came to California, the land they called "Gold Mountain." Many immigrants stayed for a few years and then returned home. Others stayed and became part of the huge workforce that built the Central Pacific Railroad.

When the railroad was completed, thousands of Chinese laborers were suddenly without work. Many went to San Francisco, the port through which most had entered the United

Chinese immigrants at the Customs House in San Francisco, waiting their turn to start a new life in America

States. By 1870, the Chinese population of the city was more than 12,000.

The Chinese suffered prejudice for many decades, however. In 1882, under pressure from Californians, Congress passed the Chinese Exclusion Act. This law banned Chinese entry into the United States. Other laws prevented Chinese from becoming citizens. It was not until 1943, during World War II, when China became an ally of the United States, that these harsh laws were ended. Today, a large Chinese community flourishes in San Francisco, and Chinatown remains a lively and vital part of the city.

6

Indians of the West

As miners, settlers, telegraph lines, and railroads moved West, Native Americans faced growing problems. The land that the U.S. government gave to the railroad companies was not empty land. It was the hunting grounds of certain Native American tribes. The mines where prospectors sought gold were on Indian lands as well. Something had to give. That something was the native people.

Relations with Whites

Wars between whites and Native Americans took place almost from the beginning of contact between the two peoples. Europeans had killed, infected, and exploited Native Americans from their first contact. Indians had often resisted, but they also had assisted white settlers.

In the West, white explorers relied on Native Americans' knowledge of the land to trace rivers and find mountain passes. White wagon trains were aided by the Native Americans they passed on the way to Oregon. Soon after the army appeared in the West, Native Americans helped soldiers by acting as scouts.

Many white pioneers, such as the mountain men and fur traders, took Native American wives. Some, like Jim Beckwourth, were adopted by their wives' tribes. William Bent and his Cheyenne wife built the trading post Bent's Fort in Colorado, near the Santa Fe Trail.

Stolen Land, Broken Promises

However, for many years, the government aimed to prevent problems between the two peoples by isolating the Indians.

"There is not among these three hundred bands of Indians one which has not suffered cruelty at the hands of either the Government or of white settlers. . . . It makes little difference . . . where one opens the record of the history of the Indians; every page and every year has its dark stain."

Helen Hunt Jackson, A Century of Dishonor, 1881

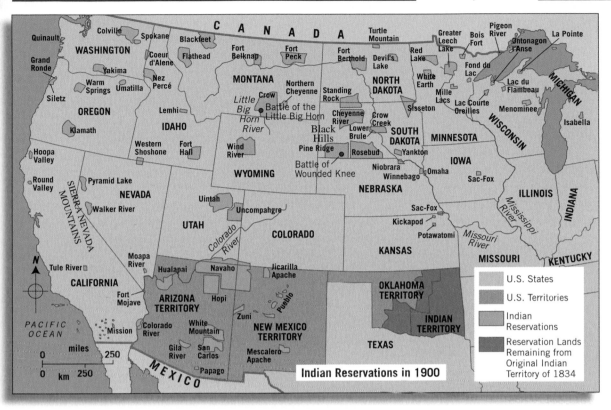

Indian Reservations in 1900

Legend:
- U.S. States
- U.S. Territories
- Indian Reservations
- Reservation Lands Remaining from Original Indian Territory of 1834

In 1834, the government passed a law that set aside the Great Plains as a gigantic Indian reservation. All United States land west of the Mississippi, except Louisiana, Missouri, and the Arkansas Territory, became Indian Territory.

This decision was made when the Plains were still seen as a desert. Over time, more and more of that land would be taken by whites. The Indians of the West soon discovered that once their land became valuable, they were no longer welcome to it.

Some estimates put the number of Indians in California at about 100,000 just before the 1849 Gold Rush. Ten years later, there may only have been about 30,000. Thousands of Native Americans were killed in a series of attacks by whites. Those few who remained were crowded onto reservations.

The Slaughter of the Buffalo

Indians of the Plains suffered another problem. The coming of the railroads threatened their way of life. Buffalo stampedes

The Indian Removal Policy of 1786 led to the founding of the first Native American reservations in the West. By 1900, reservations were scattered across the West, and the original Indian Territory, established in 1834 for the Five Civilized Tribes, had become home to more than 20 other tribes. Also by 1900, the reservation lands had been confined to a much-reduced Indian Territory and part of Oklahoma Territory. When these territories were joined in 1907 to form the state of Oklahoma, Indian Territory vanished altogether.

Buffalo slaughter became a sport in the 1860s and 1870s. These passengers on the Kansas-Pacific Railroad joined with the railroad workers in shooting buffalo from the train. The killings signaled the final end to the Plains Indians' way of life, which depended on the buffalo for survival.

were a threat to the trains and to the crews preparing the land or laying the track. The railroad companies wanted to kill buffalo to prevent these problems, and to provide meat for their laborers. The killing began in the 1860s, and increased dramatically as the demand for buffalo hides grew. Eastern industries wanted the leather to make the belts that drove their machines.

The result was a slaughter. Buffalo hunters killed buffalo by the thousands, skinning the beasts and letting the carcasses rot in the sun. One hunter, William F. Cody, shot nearly 5,000 in just 18 months. He won the name "Buffalo Bill." In 1800, about 15 million buffalo lived on the Plains. By 1883, there were hardly any.

Without their main source of food, Plains tribes suffered. The government allowed the buffalo slaughter to take place. Officials thought that without the buffalo, the Native Americans would be more likely to stay on their reservations.

The Nez Percé Fight No More Forever

The Nez Percé lived in Oregon, on the borders of Washington and Idaho. For decades they maintained good relations with whites; and they had helped Lewis and Clark to the Pacific. No white person had ever been killed by the Nez Percé. In 1855, they signed a treaty that granted them the Wallowa Valley as their permanent home. But within ten years, the growing white population of Oregon wanted the land. In 1863, the government convinced one group of Nez Percé to sign away their territory. Others in the tribe refused to acknowledge the treaty, but it was finally enforced by the United States in 1877.

Chief Joseph of the Nez Percé.

As the Indians prepared to leave, white settlers stole hundreds of their horses. The Nez Percé political leader Chief Joseph lamented, "Rather than have war, I would give up my country. . . . I would give up everything." For the next four months, Chief Joseph led his people on a forced march trying to reach Canada. They had to cross several mountains and tramp over a thousand miles (1,600 km). In the midst of this march, the Nez Percé fought several battles with four different groups of soldiers pursuing them. At every turn, the Nez Percé managed to win the battle or cleverly avoid one. But they suffered heavy losses. Finally, the Indians were trapped 30 miles (48 km) from Canada.

The Nez Percé surrendered on the understanding they would be sent to the reservation they had been promised. Chief Joseph announced, "It is cold and we have no blankets. The little children are freezing to death. . . . I am tired; my heart is sick and sad. From where the sun now stands, I will fight no more forever."

The promise was broken, and the Nez Percé were settled in poor land in the Indian Territory. Chief Joseph later met with Presidents William McKinley and Theodore Roosevelt to try and win his people the right to return to their homeland in the Wallowa Valley. He was allowed back only once, to visit the grave of his father.

"[We] have been taught to hunt and live on the game. You tell us that we must learn to farm, live in one house, and take on your ways. Suppose the people living beyond the great sea should come and tell you that you must stop farming, and kill your cattle, and take your houses and lands, what would you do? Would you not fight them?"

Gall, a Sioux chief, 1868

Fighting Back and Losing Out

In the 1860s, bloody conflict hit the Plains. The Sioux, Cheyenne, and other tribes tried to halt the growing presence of white settlers.

Opposing the Native Americans was the United States Army, stationed in several forts across the Plains. Having served in the Civil War, many soldiers were tough veterans of battle. Ten cavalry regiments were formed. The army felt that mounted troops could strike quickly when needed. Two of these cavalry regiments had African American troops, later called the "Buffalo Soldiers." There were two black infantry units as well.

Fighting first broke out in the 1860s. The Cheyenne had been forced into barren areas of Colorado. When they raided white settlements for food, a war broke out. In 1864, an army of settlers massacred between 200 and 300 Indians, including women and children, at their main camp in Colorado. Two years later, in the first Sioux War, the Sioux fought the army in the northern Plains to protest the reopening of a trail through their lands. Still, these tribes and others finally agreed to settle on reservations.

The Second Sioux War

In the early 1870s, rumors spread that there was gold in the Black Hills of South Dakota. The area was part of the Sioux reservation and was sacred to the people. The Native Americans asked the government to stop the miners from coming. Instead, government officials tried to buy the land.

In 1876, two Sioux leaders, Sitting Bull and Crazy Horse, gathered a force of between 2,000 and 2,500 angry Native Americans. On June 25, 1876, at the Little Bighorn River in what is now Montana, the Sioux force surrounded about 265 United States troops led by Colonel George Armstrong Custer. Custer's men fought to defend themselves, killing many Sioux, but were hopelessly outnumbered. All the United States troops were killed. Only a few hundred of the Sioux survived.

The news stunned the American people. Eastern newspapers reported it first on July 5, 1876, just one day after the nation's hundredth birthday. People called it "Custer's Last Stand." The army's utter defeat raised anger against the Sioux. The war continued several more years before Sitting Bull and his people escaped to Canada. Eventually, they returned to the United States and surrendered. They were sent to a reservation in what is now South Dakota.

The Sioux War was not the last of the Indian wars. The Apaches in the Southwest fought the United States because they had been moved to poor reservations and their children were stolen to be used as slaves. A small number of Apache fighters managed to elude the army for several years. They were finally defeated in 1886. Their last war leader, Geronimo, was sent off to Florida as a prisoner.

Faced by over 2,000 Sioux and Cheyenne warriors, Custer ordered the doomed men of the Seventh Cavalry Regiment to charge. The soldiers who survived the charge then retreated into a square and shot outward at the surrounding forces. Many shot their horses and used the bodies as cover. But Custer and all his men died in the Battle at the Little Bighorn.

Protests and New Policies

Some voices were raised to protest the treatment of Native Americans. In the 1870s, a young Native American teacher

Geronimo (1829–1909)

Geronimo was born in Arizona into the Chiricahua Apache tribe. His Indian name was Goyathlay. It was the Hispanics who had settled in his homelands and with whom he so bitterly fought who gave him the name Geronimo.

In 1850, by which time the United States had won the Southwest from Mexico, Geronimo's wife and children were killed by Hispanics. He became one of the Apache's leading warriors in the fight against settlers in the Southwest. He acted on behalf of his brother, Juh, a chief of the Chiricahua. Their tribe was moved to a poor reservation in eastern Arizona in 1876. For several years, Geronimo led raids against terrified white settlers and Hispanic peasants.

After a series of captures and escapes, Geronimo finally surrendered to the Americans in 1886. He and 450 members of his tribe were taken to Florida where they were confined until 1894. They were then moved to Oklahoma, where Geronimo farmed and ranched until his death. He had become a famous figure, even appearing at the 1904 World's Fair in St. Louis, Missouri.

Chief Geronimo (left, on horseback) poses for a photograph with Apache warriors shortly before his surrender in 1886.

named Susette La Flesche began speaking out for Indian rights. In 1881, Helen Hunt Jackson published a scathing attack on government Indian policy in her book *A Century of Dishonor*.

In the 1880s, the government adopted yet another new policy. The solution to the "Indian problem," it decided, was assimilation. This policy meant trying to convince Native

Helen Hunt Jackson (1830–1885) was a poet, essayist, and novelist from Massachusetts. Her study of the government's Indian policy, A Century of Dishonor, shocked many people. But nobody could deny her claim that westward expansion by white Americans had left terrible injustice and suffering in its wake.

Americans to adopt white ways of life, particularly farming. To carry out the policy, Congress passed the Dawes Act in 1887.

The law ended tribal ownership of reservation land. The land was to be divided in two ways. Each Indian who headed a family would receive a plot of 160 acres; individuals would receive smaller plots. The rest would be sold by the government to white settlers, with the proceeds of the sale to go to an educational fund for Native Americans. The policy never worked as it was intended.

Susette La Flesche (1854–1903)

Susette La Flesche was born on the Omaha Indian Reservation in Nebraska. Her Omaha name, Inshta Theamba, means "Bright Eyes." Her father was a chief of the Omaha and strongly supported the idea that Native Americans should receive a white education. One of his daughters became the first Native American woman to become a doctor. Susette went to the mission school on the reservation and then attended a school in Elizabeth, New Jersey.

La Flesche returned home to teach at the mission school. But when Chief Standing Bear of the Ponca Indians was put in jail in 1879, she decided to help. She testified in court for Standing Bear, helping him to be freed and winning an important legal victory for Native Americans.

La Flesche spent the rest of her life speaking out for Indian rights, lecturing all over the United States and in Britain. She also testified to the Senate and spoke at the White House about bettering the conditions of Indian life. Along with her husband Thomas Tibbles, a newspaper editor, La Flesche published a number of books. The *New York Herald* called one of her earliest writings about the plight of the Indians "one of the most extraordinary statements ever published in America."

Whites took all the best reservation land, and Native Americans never received any money. They were left with poor land ill suited to farming.

Slaughter at Wounded Knee

In the late 1880s, the poor, desperate Sioux of the Northern Plains embraced a new religion. Its ceremonies were called Ghost Dances, and the religion promised that the buffalo would come back and the whites would leave. The army began to worry that another revolt might be brewing. They sent men to arrest Sitting Bull in December 1890, and in the process the Sioux leader was killed.

On December 29, 1890, the Seventh Cavalry arrived at the Sioux reservation. They gathered together a group of about 350 Sioux men, women, and children at Wounded Knee Creek. They ordered the men to give up their guns, which most did. One refused, and in a struggle the gun fired. The soldiers immediately returned fire with rifles, cannons, and machine guns. Most of the Sioux were killed.

In this 1890 painting by the Western artist Frederic Remington, Native Americans of the Sioux tribe perform the Ghost Dance. Led by a Paiute Indian named Wokova, the followers of the new religion believed their rites would restore their world to the way it was before the white people came to North America. The movement united Indians from different tribes, including those who had previously fought each other.

In 1890, the Native American population received another blow. A large part of what was left of the Indian Territory, created in 1834, officially became the federal territory of Oklahoma. The area had already been opened to settlers the year before, and white people poured onto Indian land. (See map on page 61.) Once more, an agreement had been broken. And in 1907, the last remaining piece of Indian Territory was joined with Oklahoma Territory to become the state of Oklahoma.

Indian Reservations

By the 1890s, Native American tribes had lost their lands and been ravaged by disease and warfare. There were only about 250,000 Native Americans in the United States. Many people, even white supporters, believed that they would completely die out. That hasn't happened. Today there are more than 2 million Native Americans living in the United States, with the largest number in the West.

About half the native population lives on or near reservations. About 300 reservations on over 50 million acres of land are administered by the Bureau of Indian Affairs. The reservations have their own schools, colleges, and a certain amount of self-government. But because the land they were given was usually poor, these areas are still plagued by unemployment and poverty. The inhabitants are trying to find ways of making money and gaining more control over their lives. Some have successfully made claims to resources on their land, such as coal, oil, and water. Others have opened casinos to earn money that can be used to improve their peoples' way of life.

"I did not know then how much was ended. When I look back now from this high hill of my old age, I can still see the butchered women and children lying heaped and scattered all along the crooked gulch as plain as when I saw them with eyes still young. And I can see that something else died there in the bloody mud, and was buried in the blizzard. A people's dream died there. It was a beautiful dream."

Sioux Indian Black Elk, remembering Wounded Knee, Black Elk Speaks, 1932

7

The Sodbusters

During the 1860s, the Plains tribes were driven onto reservations for a simple reason. White settlers wanted their land to build farms. Until then, the "Great American Desert" had been considered unsuitable for farming. New tools began to change that view, and the growing population needed more land.

The McCormick reaper, used by these pioneers on the Plains in 1870, was introduced to the West in about 1848. The reaper was a huge help to farmers and encouraged settlement in the Western territories as a result. It rapidly increased the agricultural output of the nation, making possible huge grain exports to Europe.

New Tools, New Laws

The soil of the Plains was rich, supporting a thick growth of grass called sod. But sod was too tough for a wooden plow to break through. In 1837, John Deere invented a steel-edged plow. It could cut through the sod, making it possible to plant crops.

Another invention made it easier to harvest those crops. In 1834, Cyrus McCormick invented a reaper that speeded the process of cutting down stalks of grain. The machine worked so well that one farmer could use it to do the work of five laborers.

These machines eventually found their way onto the Plains. Other inventions followed. A mechanical harrow, invented in 1869, helped prepare the soil. After 1874, a grain drill was available to plant seeds mechanically. That same year, barbed wire fencing was invented. Until then, fencing had been a problem for farmers on the prairies where there were no trees to build wooden fences.

New laws also made it easier for people to settle the land. Bills to offer free land had been discussed in Congress for many years. Southern politicians had opposed them, fearing that the territories would be settled by a flood of Northerners who did not own slaves. With the coming of the Civil War, these Southern opponents were gone from Congress.

Congress moved quickly, and in 1862 passed the Homestead Act. The federal government measured western lands and divided them into sections of 640 acres. The Act was generous. Settlers only had to pay a ten-dollar filing fee to buy the right to 160 acres of land, or a quarter section. Then all they had to do was settle on the land and farm it for five years, after which they owned it.

Settlers on the Plains

Over the next decades, thousands took advantage of the offer. By 1900, about 400,000 families had used the Homestead Act to try to create a farm. Territories competed for settlers. People in Kansas said that Dakota was unproductive land. A Dakota newspaper editor shot back by calling one area of Kansas "a prairie where the cows give blue milk and the wind whips the long-tailed pigs to death."

When Kansas and Nebraska began to fill up, settlers moved onto the high Plains of eastern Colorado and Wyoming. This land was drier, and families

A train carriage full of recent arrivals from Europe crosses Dakota Territory in 1886. By the late 1880s, settlers were coming to the Plains not just from the eastern states but from other countries, too. Encouraged by the railroad companies, who had land to sell and trains to fill, Europeans emigrated by the thousands, hoping to find prosperity in America.

needed larger holdings to make successful farms. Congress later passed adjustments to the Homestead Act that increased the size of holdings to 640 acres and reduced the number of years homesteaders had to stay in order to own the land.

Congress took other steps aimed at helping farmers. Agricultural colleges were built, and research stations in every state experimented with new ways of farming. Over time, these steps helped to develop methods of dry farming useful on the Plains.

Homesteaders Keep Coming

Some people did not settle on homestead land but bought land from speculators or railroad companies. The railroads sent agents to Europe to convince immigrants to come to the American West, buy land, and start a farm. Almost half the settlers in Nebraska and nearly three-quarters of those in Minnesota and Wisconsin were immigrants. Many of them came from Sweden, Norway, Denmark, and Germany.

In 1889, another rush of settlement took place. The government opened up 2 million acres of land in Indian Territory (now the state of Oklahoma) to homesteaders.

After the first rush of settlers into Oklahoma Territory during 1889 and 1890, the government continued to chip away at the Indian reservation. In 1893, it opened 6 million acres of Cherokee land to white settlers. Homesteaders poured over the border to stake their claims.

Settlers were told they could not enter the land to stake their claim until noon on April 22. Some broke this rule and entered early—they were called "Sooners." About 50,000 others waited on the border. A bugle blast sounded, and the land rush began.

African Americans Move West

The Civil War ended slavery in the United States. For a brief time during the following period, called Reconstruction, African Americans in the South enjoyed new rights. Now able to vote, they sent many blacks to represent them in state capitals and in Congress. But their hopes for grants of land from the federal government were never met. Soon, whites regained control of the land and state governments. They passed laws that limited African Americans' rights. They devised a new economic system that put blacks once again under the power of white landowners.

African Americans resented their loss of rights. Many found a solution: They moved west. In 1879, thousands of African Americans began moving to the Plains. They saw it as a new exodus, like the one in the Bible, and called themselves "Exodusters."

Edwin McCabe was an African American and a successful local politician in Kansas. After the 1889 Oklahoma land rush, McCabe founded Langston City in the Oklahoma

"The quivering limbs of saddled steeds, no longer restrained by the hands that held their bridles, bounded forward simultaneously into the 'beautiful land' of Oklahoma; and wagons and carriages and buggies and prairie schooners and a whole congregation of curious equipages joined in this unparalleled race, where every starter was bound to win a prize."

Hamilton S. Wicks, Cosmopolitan, September 1889

Although African Americans gained freedom from slavery during the Civil War, their lives were not freed from prejudice and inequality. Blacks in the South found it almost impossible to acquire land for farming. Many, like this family in Kansas, moved west to African American settlements and the true independence of owning property.

The Exodusters

Henry Adams was a former slave who fought for three years in the Civil War. He set up a committee to find a place in the South where African Americans might be dealt with fairly. Hundreds of agents gathered information. All seemed to have the same findings: Former slaves were being mistreated across the region.

The committee then asked the government "to help us out of our distress, or protect us in our rights and privileges." Their petitions were ignored. Finally, the committee decided to move their members out of the South. In 1879, a huge number of people began the slow and difficult migration to the West.

In the exodus of 1879 alone, between 20,000 and 40,000 former slaves moved to Kansas and other parts of the West, led by Benjamin "Pap" Singleton. The governor of Kansas welcomed the Exodusters. But these new settlers were not always welcome. One group was driven out of a Nebraska city, and others met prejudice along the way. Many of the settlements faced collapse during the first cold winter, but a huge relief effort in Kansas made sure that no one froze or starved to death. A large number of the settlements went on to grow and prosper.

"I could not agree with my husband that any good could come out of such a country, but . . . October 1, 1879, saw us . . . bound for the 'Promised Land.' . . . To say I wept bitterly would but faintly express the ocean of tears I shed . . ."

Mrs W. B. Catton, homesteader

Territory, which he aimed to set aside for African Americans. He sent agents to the South to recruit settlers. Other cities followed, and by 1910 there were 30 towns in Oklahoma that were home to African Americans.

Life on the Plains

Everything about moving west was hard: the trip, building a home, creating and working a farm, and enduring long, hot summers and cold, windy winters. Some settlers found it difficult to leave their homes in the East.

Getting a farm started was especially grueling work. For this the homesteaders earned the nickname "sodbusters." Even with a steel plow, they needed several oxen and strong people to break the sod. If they didn't have a grain drill, they made holes for the seeds using an ax.

Dugouts and Soddies

When settlers arrived on the Plains, they had to build a house. Clumps of trees grew alongside streams and rivers, but they did not provide enough lumber to build a house. The settlers found alternatives. If their land had a hill, they dug homes called "dugouts" into the side. Often the only sign that a dugout existed was an iron chimney poking through the top of the hill.

However, the Plains are mainly flat, and most of the settlers built houses from blocks of sod, or turf. The blocks were cut out of the ground in pieces about three or four inches (8 to 10 cm) thick, a foot (30 cm) wide and two or three feet (60 to 90 cm) long. The walls were built in layers, like brick walls, and were usually two or three blocks thick. The cracks between the sod blocks were filled with loose soil to keep out the wind and pests. Wooden beams made a frame for the roof, which was then covered with grass and turf. These sod houses, or "soddies," were cool in summer and warm in winter.

Both dugouts and soddies were miserable in the rain, however. Water leaked through the roofs and turned the earthen floors to mud. Settlers looked forward to the day they could afford to buy lumber shipped in from the East and build a wooden house.

A sod house near Coburg, Nebraska, 1887.

The Grange promoted farming as vital to the nation's economy, and campaigned for agricultural reforms to protect its members.

"Burn down your cities and leave our farms, and your cities will spring up again as if by magic; but destroy our farms and the grass will grow in the streets of every city in the country."

William Jennings Bryan, 1896

The settlers planted vegetable gardens with beans and peas, squash, turnips, cabbage, and potatoes. They kept a few cows for milk and to make butter, chickens for eggs, and hogs for meat. The main crops were grains: corn in the eastern Plains and wheat toward the west.

The harvest was long and tiring, and all farm work was subject to natural disasters. Too much rain could lead to rot. Too little meant drought and withered crops. And when the grasses or fields were dry, prairie fires swept through quickly. At the hint of smoke, families would spring into action. In 1874, a different plague struck Kansas. Thousands of grasshoppers swarmed from the Rocky Mountains over the Plains, destroying crops.

Life on the Plains was lonely as well. Farms were far apart and needed constant work. There was no time for travel or social life. Many people simply could not take the loneliness or the hard work, and half the homesteaders failed to stay the course. Some remained in the West, moving to cities. Others packed their belongings in "mover wagons" and headed back east.

Farmers Fight Back

Plains farmers had to borrow money to buy the machines they used. When grain prices fell, their incomes dropped and they couldn't repay the loans. Many took out mortgages on their farms to raise money. They used those funds to buy more land and equipment, hoping that by growing more grain they could earn enough to pay off their loans.

At the same time, farmers were angry at the railroad companies. They argued that the railroads charged too much to transport their grain to markets. In 1867, farmers formed an organization called the Patrons of Husbandry, or the Grange.

At first, it was meant as a social organization for farmers. Soon, however, Grangers began to fight for lower shipping prices.

Later, in the 1880s, other groups followed. African American farmers created the National Colored Farmers' Alliance. Southern farmers formed the Southern Alliance, bringing together about 4 million farmers. In the West, the largest body was the National Farmers' Alliance of the Northwest.

The Populists

In the late 1880s, the Plains were hit by several years of drought. Crops failed and many farmers lost their land to the banks that held the mortgages. The people who worked in the alliances felt that having political power was the best way to help the farmers. In 1891, they formed the Populist party. Speakers like Mary Elizabeth Lease campaigned heavily in farming regions.

The Populists staged a convention in Omaha, Nebraska, in 1892. They backed a wide variety of reforms, many to help farmers. In the presidential election, the Populist candidate won 10 percent of the popular vote, a strong showing for a new party. The Populist party received great support in the Plains and other western states. Three Populists became governors, five became senators, and about 1,500 were elected to state legislatures.

The next year, a terrible recession struck the United States. About one-fifth of all workers lost their jobs. A huge debate arose about how to solve the economic problem. The Populists supported a Democrat, newspaper editor and former Congressman William Jennings Bryan of

Mary Elizabeth Lease (1850–1933)

Mary Elizabeth Lease became a fiery speaker on behalf of farmers. Enemies called her "the Kansas Pythoness." Admirers named her "our Queen Mary."

Born Mary Clyens in Pennsylvania of Irish immigrant parents, she moved to Kansas at age 20 to take a job as a teacher. She then married Charles Lease and, with her husband, struggled to start a family farm.

In the 1890s, she began to speak out on behalf of farmers. A lively speaker, Lease roused the crowd with her advice that farmers should "raise less corn and more hell." In 1892, when Chicago held the huge and popular World's Columbian Exposition, she was chosen as the speaker on Kansas Day.

Lease became a rising figure in the Populist party. In 1892, she was named the Populist candidate for the U.S. Senate from Kansas, where women could vote. She lost the election, though, and soon broke with other Populist leaders. She later moved to New York and took up other causes, including women's right to vote.

Nebraska, who wanted to take steps to help farmers and other poor, working people. At the 1896 Democratic party convention, Bryan gave a powerful speech and won the Democratic nomination for president. But he was beaten in the election by Republican William McKinley. The power of the Populists, already weakened in the South, soon declined in the West as well.

Preserving the Land

A passenger coach tours Yellowstone Park in 1910, when tourism and wilderness preservation were still fairly new ideas.

As homesteaders flooded to the Plains and the West filled up, certain people began to worry about losing the nation's natural wonders to farmers and ranchers. In 1870, some explorers suggested to Congress that an area in northwestern Wyoming be set aside as a national park. Yellowstone came into existence in 1872. It was followed in 1890 by Yosemite National Park in California.

Today, there are more than 50 national parks in the United States. Around 4 percent of the nation's land is managed by the National Park Service. In addition to national parks, this includes many historic sites, monuments, rivers, and other nature preserves. Some of the world's most famous and beautiful places are included in the park system. The National Park Service gives access to these areas to millions of people every year, providing roads and amenities for visitors. But its job is also to preserve the wilderness. Some areas within the parks remain as they were before the white settlers came West.

8

Legends of the West

The last decades of the 1800s saw the birth of some of the most enduring images of the West. These were the years when cowboys drove thousands of cattle over the open range. This was the time of the great Oklahoma land rush. It was the period when men rode down the wild waters of the Colorado River and sent back word about the Grand Canyon.

These images have been engraved in Americans' minds by books, movies, and television. However, they tell only part of the story.

The Cattle Kingdom

Before the Civil War, the Anglo settlers of Texas had taken up the Hispanic practice of herding cattle. Owners branded their cattle with a mark to show ownership. Then they let the cattle roam over the open land.

After the Gold Rush created a new market for meat, some cattle owners drove herds to California. Others drove their herds east to New Orleans. During the Civil War, the Confederate army created a huge demand for beef. But when Union forces seized the Mississippi, cattle could not be moved out of Texas. By the time the Civil War ended in 1865, Texans had about five million cattle on the open range.

Three other changes outside Texas had also taken place. First, cities in the North and East were growing, and so was the people's appetite for meat. Second, Chicago had become a major center for shipping cattle to the eastern market. Third, as the Plains became farmland, the area could no longer support herds of cattle. Chicago's supply of cattle was disappearing.

Moving the Cattle

The question was, how could the Texas beef reach Chicago? It was worth the cattle owner's while to find an answer. Cattle that was worth $4 a head in Texas sold for $40 in Chicago. The answer was to move the cattle north through Oklahoma and into Missouri or Kansas. They could be taken to a railroad, which would haul the cattle off to Chicago. The first attempt came in 1866, when several cattle owners drove thousands of cattle north to Sedalia, Missouri. They suffered many losses in the rough country. They also ran into angry farmers who protested when the cattle trampled their fields. But when they sold the cattle, they made good profits.

Joseph McCoy came up with a way to avoid problems with farmers: Bring the cattle to some point west of the farmers and then ship them by rail to Chicago. McCoy approached the small town of Abilene, Kansas, where people agreed to his plan. He worked with Jesse Chisholm, a Native American, who blazed a trail north from Texas to Abilene. Then McCoy promoted Abilene to the cattle ranchers in Texas and to the railroad companies in the East.

In 1867, McCoy's dream became a reality. He had invented something new: the Long Drive. The cattle came

The Long Drive

Whether on the Chisholm Trail to Abilene, the Shawnee Trail to Missouri, or the Goodnight-Loving Trail to Denver, Long Drives were the same. The process began in the spring with the roundup. Cowboys hired by the cattle owners rode the Texas range to gather all the cattle together. The cowboys branded calves with their owner's mark. Then most of the year-old males, called steers, were taken from the herd to be driven north.

The drives lasted about three months. There was one cowboy for about 250 animals. The rest of the crew included a wrangler, who cared for extra horses; a cook, who rode in a chuck wagon; and a trail boss. They drove the cattle over dry, dusty plains and through rivers. When the water was swift, it could wash an animal downstream. Cowboys were in the saddle as long as 18 hours a day, always on the watch for something, such as a clap of thunder or a thoughtless gunshot, that could set off a stampede. It was exhausting and frustrating work.

About one-eighth of the cowboys were Hispanics. They were experienced in the work and knew how to handle the cattle. The cowboys used the equipment and techniques developed in Spanish colonial days. Over their legs, they wore leather chaps, which came from the Spanish *chaparajos*. They used a lariat—from the Spanish *la reata*—to rope calves for branding and guide steers on the trail. They rode sturdy Spanish mustang horses—from the Spanish *mesteños*—as they did their work.

A quarter of the men were African Americans. They included Bill Pickett, who invented the rodeo event called bulldogging. The bulldogger jumps off his horse, grabs a steer's horns, and wrestles it to the ground. Most rodeo events developed from skills used by cowboys herding cattle.

Cattle move north on the Long Drive from Texas.

> "The cattle congregated into a mass of unmanageable animals, milling and lowing in their fever and thirst. . . . No sooner was the milling stopped than they would surge hither and yon, sometimes half a mile, as ungovernable as the waves of an ocean. . . . They finally turned back over the trail, and the utmost efforts of every man in the outfit failed to check them."
>
> *Cowboy Andy Adams, describing the difficulties of the Long Drive*

over the 600-mile (965-km) Chisholm Trail to Abilene, where a railroad line was built to meet them. (See map on page 85.) About 35,000 head of cattle went east by rail that year, and about 75,000 the next.

Often, the Long Drives included cattle belonging to more than one owner. Money would be divided among the owners after the cattle were sold. The cattle were Texas longhorns, descended from the animals brought to North America by the Spanish. They did not provide great quantities of meat. But they were tough beasts that could live in hard country.

The meat companies that moved live steers to the East had to pay for their shipping by the pound. They wanted to ship just the meat, but needed a way to prevent that meat from spoiling. In 1868, meat packer George Hammond developed a rail car full of ice. The refrigerator car made him huge profits.

Abilene became a boom town, but its monopoly on the cattle business lasted less than five years. As the years passed, the homesteading farmers reached Abilene, making it difficult to drive the cattle there. Other Kansas towns tried to win their share of the cattle business. Wichita and Dodge City became the new cattle towns. Because they were farther south, cattle owners did not have to drive their herds as far.

The End of an Era

The era of the cattle drives was shortlived. Homesteaders built farms in Texas, closing parts of the open range. Barbed wire fences on the southern Plains made driving cattle more difficult. However, the destruction of the buffalo herds opened the northern Plains for other animals. Soon, some cattle owners were keeping their herds farther north, closer to the rail lines.

Other cattle owners responded by taking a different approach. They began to invest in better quality cattle that were meatier than the longhorns. With more money invested in their herds, they wanted to care for them year round. Ranchers began to fence their land, too, to keep their cattle in. The open range was finished.

The Developing West

The West had become a region of many new peoples. African Americans had become cowboys and soldiers, homesteaders and mine workers. Chinese worked in mines and built railroads. They tended farms and worked in cities. Hispanics lived mostly in California, the Southwest, and Texas, where they filled many working roles. Native Americans had been pushed to the margins of western life.

Relations among all these groups were not always smooth and peaceful. White workers complained that Asian Americans worked for less and took away their jobs. This anger could boil over into violence, as it did at a Wyoming coal mine in 1885, when 28 Chinese miners were killed by white miners.

African Americans also met prejudice. Edwin McCabe's efforts to establish communities of blacks in Oklahoma resulted in a backlash from whites. The government of the territory, and later the state, was controlled by whites, who put in place a policy of strict segregation.

On the other hand, women enjoyed more rights in the West than they did in other parts of the country. Wyoming Territory gave women the right to vote and hold office in 1869. Washington Territory did so as well, although the right was taken away in its first state constitution. Utah had a women's newspaper, which began publishing in 1872. By 1919, only four western states had not given women the vote.

Women went to the voting station in Cheyenne, Wyoming Territory, to vote in the 1888 presidential election. It would be 22 years before the Nineteenth Amendment of 1920 gave women all over the United States the right to vote.

Creating the Legend

By the late 1800s, the West had developed a certain image in the minds of Americans. Relations between Native Americans and whites were largely peaceful at this time, but the Indian wars of the 1860s and 1870s had left a strong mark. One reason was the death in 1876 of Colonel George Custer, who had been a popular and colorful Indian fighter. After he perished at Little Bighorn, his wife wrote three books that portrayed her husband as a great soldier, a perfect husband, and a model man. She built a myth that has lasted more than a century after his death.

Other popular books produced images of the West. In the late 1800s, romantic stories were published about cowboys and other Western figures. These books, known as "dime novels," were cheap, exciting, and easy to read. Stories of one cowboy hero, called "Deadwood Dick," first appeared in 1877.

Nat Love (1854–1921)

The African American cowboy Nat Love claimed in his autobiography that he was the source of the fictional figure "Deadwood Dick."

Love was born into slavery in Davidson County, Tennessee. After the Civil War, he went West to seek his fortune and escape discrimination. In his own words, Love lived a life "wild, reckless, and free, afraid of nothing." He drove cattle for a living, herding thousands of animals over long stretches of the country.

By 1890, the days of the cattle drives were over, and Love became a Pullman porter for the railroad. In 1907, he wrote his autobiography, becoming the only black cowboy to write a full length book about his experiences. In *The Life and Adventures of Nat Love, Better Known in the Cattle Country as "Deadwood Dick,"* Love tells of his amazing adventures. He describes how a tribe of Native Americans adopted him, and how he had to ride 12 hours to escape another group. Love's book is full of scrapes with death, not all necessarily true.

The outlaws of the West, like Jesse James and Billy the Kid, also became part of the legend. So, too, did the lawmen Wild Bill Hickock and Wyatt Earp.

The End of the Frontier

In 1890, although the image still flourished, the Census Bureau of the federal government made a surprising announcement. The frontier, it said, no longer existed. The bureau defined the frontier as the line between white and Native American settlements. As the nineteenth century progressed, the frontier line had moved steadily westward. And with settlers and cattle ranchers working on all of the Plains, it was decided that there was no longer any such line. But the frontier had never really been a definite line. It was the region where different peoples had lived together, both at war and in peace.

Before 1812, there were no states west of the Mississippi River. Only one hundred years later, the entire area from the Mississippi to the Pacific Ocean had been organized into 22 new states. By 1912, the frontier had truly disappeared.

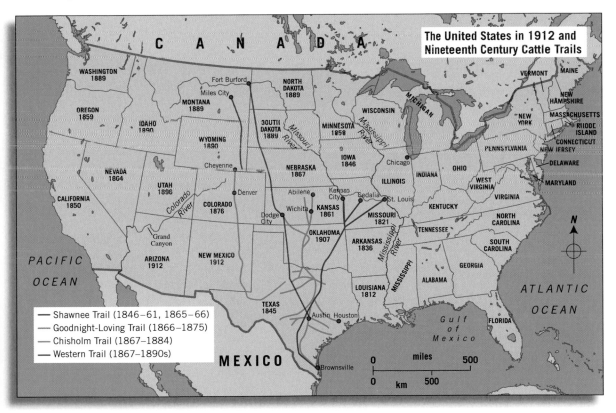

The United States in 1912 and Nineteenth Century Cattle Trails

— Shawnee Trail (1846–61, 1865–66)
— Goodnight-Loving Trail (1866–1875)
— Chisholm Trail (1867–1884)
— Western Trail (1867–1890s)

85

The Wild West Show

William F. Cody, known as "Buffalo Bill," created his own legend by turning his real life experience of the West into a worldwide entertainment. As a young man, he had been a Pony Express rider, and later he killed thousands of buffalo for the railroads. He was also chief of scouts for the Fifth U.S. Cavalry during the Sioux Wars.

In 1883, Cody assembled a crew of talented people from the West. His Wild West Show drew huge crowds attracted to performances of buffalo hunts, stagecoach robberies, and gunfights. There were also displays of trick shooting, horse riding, and cattle roping. The show was a great success for many years, traveling all over the country and even to Europe.

One star of the Wild West Show was sharpshooter Annie Oakley. Superb with a rifle, she dazzled the crowds with her speed and marksmanship. Native Americans also starred in the show, dressed in their finest traditional clothes and mounted on beautiful horses. The Wild West Show did much to promote the image of frontier life that we still have today.

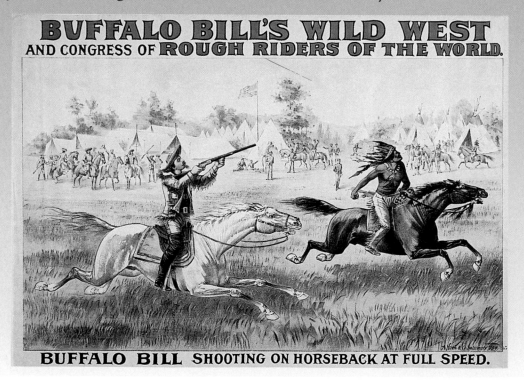

BUFFALO BILL'S WILD WEST AND CONGRESS OF ROUGH RIDERS OF THE WORLD.

BUFFALO BILL SHOOTING ON HORSEBACK AT FULL SPEED.

Conclusion

At the beginning of the 1800s, the United States acquired its first piece of land west of the Mississippi. By the end of the same century, the expanded western territories had become 19 new states. Many large towns had grown up. In 1890, the proportion of Westerners who lived in towns with a population of 10,000 or more was larger than that of people in the Midwest and South.

As the population of the West grew, the character of the region changed. Where Native Americans and buffalo had once lived, farmers now harvested wheat and ranchers grazed cattle. Where the Spanish had once ruled, Spanish-speaking people now lived under American law. Native American fishing peoples of the Northwest had given way to farmers, lumber companies, and cities.

In this short period of time, the huge expanse of the West had ceased to be a separate and unknown place. United States territory now stretched across the continent of North America. By 1912, Oklahoma, Arizona and New Mexico had also joined the Union. The westward expansion of the United States of America was complete.

The idea of Manifest Destiny captured the imagination of the American people and was often expressed in art of the period. This romantic painting by John Gast, called "American Progress," idealizes western expansion. White settlers are seen moving west, taking with them new forms of transportation, agriculture, and technology.

Glossary

alliance An agreement between two or more people, groups, or countries to side together during a conflict. Countries or people with such an agreement become allies.

annex To take ownership of another nation or add territory to a nation.

assembly A group of people gathered together. People elected to make laws in the United States formed assemblies that were part of local governments.

cavalry Soldiers who fight on horseback.

constitution The basic plan and principles of a government.

Continental Divide The point in the Rocky Mountains from which all rivers to the east flow to the Gulf of Mexico and all rivers to the west flow to the Pacific Ocean.

democracy A system in which people are their own authority rather than being ruled over by a king or queen. In a democratic system, people vote on decisions, or elect representatives to vote for them.

economics To do with the production and use of goods and services, and the system of money that is used for the flow of goods and services.

federal To do with the central, or national, government of a country rather than the regional, or state, governments.

frontier The edge of something known or settled. In North America, the frontier for white settlers moved as they themselves moved west onto new lands.

Hispanics Spanish-speaking people living in North America who are descended from Spanish settlers, and often also from the Native Americans and African Americans with whom the Spanish mixed.

immigrant A person who has left the country of his or her birth and come to live in another country.

infantry Soldiers who fight on foot.

legislature The branch of government that makes laws.

migration Movement from one place to another in search of a new place to live.

missionary A person who goes to another country (or to another part of his or her own country) to convert the people there to his or her religion, and sometimes to help the poor or sick.

mortgage A loan taken out using property owned by the borrower as a guarantee that the loan will be repaid. If it is not, the lender can take possession of the property.

ordinance A government regulation.

outpost A base in a foreign country or outlying area that is used for military defense or for trading.

petition A paper signed by people asking a government body to take some action.

plantation A farm where crops, such as tobacco or sugarcane, are grown and where the work is done by large teams of workers. In the past, these workers were often slaves.

policy A plan or way of doing things that is decided on, and then used in managing situations, making decisions, or tackling problems.

recession A time when the economy of a country or region slows down, resulting in businesses cutting back on production and workers losing their jobs.

reservation An area of land set aside for Native American tribes whose homelands had been taken or reduced by white settlement.

segregation The policy of keeping people from different racial groups separate. It usually means that one group has fewer rights than another.

speculator A person who buys something, risking that it will increase in value and later be sold for more money than was paid for it.

technology The knowledge and ability that improves ways of doing practical things. A person performing a task using any tool, from a wooden spoon to the most complicated computer, is applying technology.

telegraph A communication system that uses electricity to send coded signals along wires.

treaty An agreement reached between two or more groups or countries after discussion and negotiation.

tribe A social group or community that shares traditions and ways of life. Native American tribes are part of larger groups called "peoples." These peoples often share a common language.

veteran A person who served for a long time at a job, particularly in the military, or who served on a specific campaign or expedition.

Time Line

1763	Britain defeats France in French and Indian War.
	British Proclamation bans white settlement west of Appalachians.
1769	Spain orders missions and forts built in California.
1775	Daniel Boone clears Wilderness Road.
1785	Land Ordinance organizes land and settlement in Northwest.
1787	Northwest Ordinance creates territories in Northwest.
1792	Kentucky becomes a state.
1796	Tennessee becomes a state.
1800	Harrison Land Act.
1803	Louisiana Purchase.
	Ohio becomes a state.
1804–06	Lewis and Clark expedition.
1806	Expedition of Zebulon Pike.
1812	Louisiana becomes a state.
1812–14	War of 1812.
1813–14	Creek War.
1814	Treaty of Greenville.
1816	Indiana becomes a state.
1817	Mississippi becomes a state.
1818	Illinois becomes a state.
1819	Alabama becomes a state.
1820	Expedition of Stephen Long.
1821	Mexico wins independence from Spain.
	Missouri becomes a state.
1822	First Anglos settle in Texas.
1830	Indian Removal Act.
1836	Texas wins independence from Mexico.
	Arkansas becomes a state.
1838–39	Cherokee Indians moved west along Trail of Tears.
1842	First mass migration along Oregon Trail.
1845	Texas becomes a state.
1846	Iowa becomes a state.
1846	Oregon Treaty between United States and Britain.
1846–47	Mormon migration to Utah.

1846–48	Mexican War.
1848	Treaty of Guadalupe Hidalgo.
1849	California Gold Rush begins.
1850	California becomes a state.
1853	Gadsden Purchase.
1858	First journey of Overland Express stagecoach.
	Minnesota becomes a state.
1859	Oregon becomes a state.
1860–61	Pony Express provides transcontinental mail service.
1861	Transcontinental telegraph lines completed.
	Kansas becomes a state.
1862	Congress passes Homestead Act.
1864	Nevada becomes a state.
1865–68	First Sioux War.
1866	First cattle drive to Sedalia, Missouri.
1867	Farmers organize alliance known as "The Grange."
	Congress approves purchase of Alaska.
	Nebraska becomes a state.
1869	Transcontinental railroad completed.
1872	United States' first national park created at Yellowstone, Wyoming.
1875–76	Second Sioux War.
1876	Battle at the Little Bighorn.
	Colorado becomes a state.
1887	Dawes Act ends tribal ownership of reservations.
1889	Land rush in Oklahoma.
	Montana, North Dakota, South Dakota, and Washington become states.
1890	Massacre at Wounded Knee.
	Oklahoma Territory created.
	Idaho and Wyoming become states.
	Government proclaims end of frontier.
1891	Populist party formed.
1896	Utah becomes a state.
1907	Oklahoma becomes a state.
1912	Arizona and New Mexico become states.

Further Reading

Emert, Phyllis R. *All That Glitters: Men and Women of the Gold and Silver Rushes* (Perspectives on History Series). Carlisle, MA: Discovery Enterprises, 1995.

Herb, Angela. *Beyond the Mississippi: Early Westward Expansion of the United States*. New York: Lodestar, 1996.

Hoig, Stan. *Night of the Cruel Moon: Cherokee Removal and the Trail of Tears*. New York: Facts On File, 1996.

Katz, William Loren. *Black Pioneers: An Untold Story*. Golden, CO: Atheneum, 1999.

Laughlin, Rosemary. *The Great Iron Link: The Building of the Central Pacific Railroad* (Great Events Series). Greensboro, NC: Morgan Reynolds, 1996.

Pelta, Kathy. *Cattle Trails* (American Trails Series). Austin, TX: Raintree Steck-Vaughn, 1998.

———. *Trails to the West* (American Trails Series). Austin, TX: Raintree Steck-Vaughn, 1998.

Sanford, William R., and Carl R. Green. *Bill Pickett: African American Rodeo Cowboy* (Legendary Heroes of the Wild West Series). Springfield, NJ: Enslow, 1997.

Stefoff, Rebecca. *Women Pioneers* (American Profiles Series). New York: Facts On File, 1996.

Toht, David W. *Sodbuster* (American Pathfinder Series). Minneapolis, MN: Lerner, 1996.

Websites

Buffalo Bill Historical Center – Includes artifacts and information from the Plains Indian Museum and the Buffalo Bill Museum.
http://www.bbhc.org

The Spanish Missions of California – Information about California missions and the people who lived in them; an educational website created by high school students.
http://library.thinkquest.org/3615/

Bibliography

Ambrose, Stephen E. *Undaunted Courage*. New York: Touchstone, 1996.

Bataille, Gretchen M., ed. *Native American Women: A Biographical Dictionary*. New York: Garland Publishing, 1993.

Bohlander, Dick, ed. *World Explorers and Discoverers*. New York: Macmillan, 1992.

Colbert, David, ed. *Eyewitness to America*. New York: Pantheon Books, 1997.

Commager, Henry Steele, and Allan Nevins, eds. *Witness to America*. New York: Barnes and Noble Books, 1996.

Danzer, Gerald A., et al. *The Americans*. Evanston, IL: McDougal Littell, 1998.

Foner, Eric. *A Short History of Reconstruction*. New York: Harper & Row, 1990.

Hoxie, Frederick E. *Encyclopedia of North American Indians*. Boston: Houghton Mifflin, 1996.

Jennings, Francis. *The Founders of America*. New York: W. W. Norton, 1993.

Katcher, Philip. *US Cavalry on the Plains 1850-90*. London: Osprey Publishing, 1985.

Katz, William Loren. *Black People Who Made the Old West*. Trenton, NJ: Africa World Press, 1992.

————. *Eyewitness: A Living Documentary of the African American Contribution to American History*, rev. ed. New York: Touchstone, 1995.

Milner, Clyde A. II, et al., eds. *The Oxford History of the American West*. New York: Oxford University Press, 1994.

Morgan, Ted. *A Shovel of Stars: The Making of the American West—1800 to the Present*. New York: Touchstone, 1996.

Moynihan, Ruth Barnes, et al., eds. *Second to None: A Documentary History of American Women*. Lincoln, NE: University of Nebraska Press, 1993.

Peavy, Linda, and Ursula Smith. *Pioneer Women: The Lives of Women on the Frontier*. Norman, OK: University of Oklahoma Press, 1996.

Philips, Charles, and Alan Axelrod. *Encyclopedia of the American West*. New York: Macmillan Reference USA, 1996.

Stratton, Joanna L. *Pioneer Women: Voices from the Kansas Frontier*. New York: Touchstone, 1981.

Takaki, Ronald. *Strangers from a Different Shore*. New York: Penguin, 1989.

Index